ditchthe

BITCH

stigma

embrace your inner badass

ditch the BITCH stigma

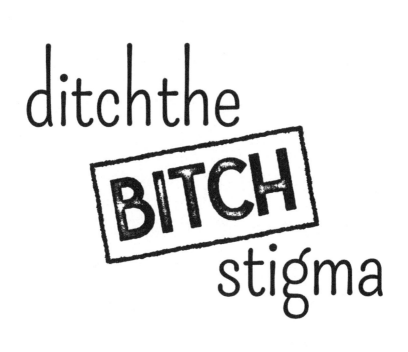

embrace your inner badass

KALI WILLIAMS

BRAZEN
INK
PRESS

Published by Brazen Ink Press

www.BrazenInkPress.com

San Jose, CA

Cover design by Hannah Portello-Swagel

Book design by Alex Head / Draft Lab

ISBN: 978-1-7340322-1-5

Printed in the United States of America

Contents

Introduction

"WHY DO YOU HAVE TO be such a bitch about this?"

My tall, imposing roommate was standing at the bottom of the stairs blocking my way. He had been angrily explaining why he wanted to stay in his room in the apartment we shared with two other roommates who had recently announced they were moving out.

"I've already told you," he continued. "This place is close to my work, it's cheap and I want to live here. So let's just look for two people to replace them."

I had already decided that I wanted to take over the whole apartment and use the extra rooms as office space for my growing business. The cheap rent meant I could afford it. Besides, I had already lived there for three years and was on great terms with the landlords while this roommate had just moved in a few months ago. There was no reason I shouldn't be awarded the whole place.

But for the last couple of weeks, this guy had been trying to intimidate me into letting him stay. I didn't know him very well, and the aggressive, angry, entitled tone he kept taking wasn't helping his case.

Then, when I heard those magic words—"Why do you have to be such a bitch about this?"—a sort of clarity and calm took over, and I simply said, "If taking care of my own needs above yours makes me a bitch, then so be it," and pushed past him to get out of the house. I made the call to the landlords that day, and he was out by the following month.

That was the moment I completely changed my relationship to being called a bitch.

I'm what's known as a "difficult woman." Before that, I was a "difficult girl." Among other things, I've been called a militant feminist, a laser beam of intensity, and, of course, a bitch.

Women spend an exorbitant amount of energy navigating the unspoken cultural expectation to be confident, outspoken, and independent without crossing over the constantly shifting line into "bitch" territory. The fear that drives so many of us to spend all this unnecessary energy is what I call the Bitch Stigma. My hope is that this book will help women learn to ditch the Bitch Stigma and embrace their inner badass. More on what that means, what it looks like, and how to achieve it, is coming up.

What Is the Bitch Stigma?

The Bitch Stigma (which I'll sometimes refer to as BS because, let's face it, that's what it is), refers to the very real fear of the equally real potential consequences women can face simply for being assertive. Any time a woman tries to assert herself, assert her boundaries, assert her authority, or assert her self-respect, she risks being labeled bitchy, bossy, or domineering. These risks drive the Bitch Stigma, which bubbles up to undermine women's confidence, creating self-doubt and encouraging self-defeating behaviors.

This sexist sentiment says that women who are described as bitchy, bossy, or domineering can't get ahead and won't be liked. Women are supposed to wait for other people to give us value and respect our boundaries. So, if you're a strong, self-assured woman, you're breaking the unwritten rules, and disrupting the status quo, and that makes people nervous and uncomfortable.

The Bitch Stigma is a way of keeping women controlled through fear of consequences for simply being assertive and direct.

It can be a conundrum because, as women, standing tall can end up making us feel small and vulnerable. We put on our armor, we put on our resting bitch faces. We go out into the world to speak directly. We try not to back down or bow down. But it's scary.

We don't know what the consequences will be when we behave like the strong women we are. And there *can* be consequences to standing up for ourselves. We are still living in a world that doesn't consistently support strong behavior from women, and that's not going to change overnight. We could be rejected, we could spark violence, or we could even lose our livelihoods and the relationships that matter most to us.

So instead of risking all that, we cruise along with our heads down and hope that people will think the best of us and that everything will work out on its own.

It's not working, it's not enough, and it shouldn't be acceptable anymore.

"You'll often hear people say, 'Well, you're helping women find their voices,' and I fundamentally disagree with that, because women don't need to find a voice. They need to feel empowered to use it, and people need to be encouraged to listen."

—MEGHAN MARKLE, HER ROYAL HIGHNESS

Women are told to be many things throughout our lives. Agreeable. Soft. Nurturing. Encouraging. But above all, there's one thing we're told to avoid being: a bitch. This book is going to blow that bullshit out of the water.

The Bitch Stigma is the pushback that women get when we stand in our power, when we set boundaries, when we communicate directly, and when we pursue our own ambitions. These are all perfectly healthy things for a human being to do, but thanks to deep-seated gender expectations, they're often reserved for men. When women do these things, it's considered inappropriate, and that's what creates the Bitch Stigma.

As a result, women spend an inordinate amount of time managing our tones and managing others' expectations and misconceptions. We live our lives in fear of being labeled bitches. Of being shamed and mocked for being "difficult."

Who Is This Book For?

I've been using the word "women" a lot so far, so let me take a minute to be clear about who I mean. My good friend, Marcia Baczynski, founder of Good Girl Recovery Program[1], captures it perfectly, so with her permission, I've adapted her words to explain who this book is for.

This book is for women and people socialized as and/or identifying as women, no matter their race, religious orientation, socioeconomic background, or anything else. I am explicitly including trans women, cis women, straight women, queer women, women who feel kind of wobbly about being a woman, non-binary people who have been treated by the world as a girl or a woman, and gender-fluid people who experience a significant part of their days navigating female expectations.

To reduce friction while you're reading, I'll be using the umbrella term "women," but I'm referring to everyone who identifies as a woman and not just those born with two X chromosomes. I'll use a lot of binary terminology around gender in this book because, while gender is not and should not be binary, society's behavioral expectations are still very much so.

This book is for the women who realize that the expected softness isn't working for us. As we move through life doing the "right" thing—namely, being polite and behaving ourselves—we are still not making progress in our careers, and we're not being respected by our peers, colleagues, friends, or loved ones.

This book is for the women who've realized that what we're doing isn't working and our best option is to try something else.

It's for women who are ready for a new approach to old problems. If we're not going to get what we need by being polite, we might as well try to get it by not being polite. Sure, there may be sacrifices, but we may be sacrificing things that don't matter in the first place.

Who Am I to Teach You to Be a Bitch?

I've been an advocate for women being badasses for the last twenty years. I'm passionate about helping women let go of their fear of being labeled a bitch and to spend less time prioritizing what other people think of them.

Surprisingly, my focus on women's empowerment comes with a twist, in that my expertise comes from twelve years working as a professional dominatrix. In other words, I was a professional bitch. I was someone others came to for help shedding gendered expectations and exploring social taboos of a very wide variety. Alongside my dominatrix work, I was also (and still am) a BDSM teacher and kink coach.

What is BDSM? It stands for bondage/discipline, dominance/submission, sado-masochism.

What is kink? It's a more overarching term to include all creative and "non-standard" exploration of sexuality.

My work as a dominatrix allowed me the space to learn how to speak with strength, enforce boundaries, and to feel powerful in a way that the world had told me I wasn't allowed to. My biggest discovery over the years was that the techniques I used to help women claim more confidence in the bedroom, get their needs met, and express themselves were techniques they could—and did—use to get their needs met in other areas of their lives.

It turns out that the techniques required to approach difficult topics are universal. The strategies are similar, whether we're building confidence in the bedroom, the boardroom, or any other room.

Once I made that discovery, I started translating the lessons I've learned and shared in the kink world into broader techniques for women to use in every aspect of our lives.

Because, despite common misconceptions, the reality is that BDSM is not about anger or violence or how you look. It's not even always about sex. It's about psychology. The way I approach it, BDSM is all about power dynamics, because in this crazy, out-of-control world we live in, it can be really seductive to create a safe space where you can either give up or take control, consensually, consciously, conscientiously, and with purpose.

Domination wasn't at all about sex for me, either. It was about feeling in control and being able to truly embrace my power.

My domination work was about helping both myself and my clients confront gendered stereotypes and gendered restrictions. It gave me an opportunity to undo my own early programming that said that women are not assertive or sexual or powerful. It allowed my clients—mostly men—the opportunity to be vulnerable and submissive, distinctly "feminine traits." In this space, they weren't required to have all the answers or to be the driving force of every interaction.

How did it work? To start, let me be clear that I have never professionally engaged in traditional sex acts. Instead, when I was working as a dominatrix, my clients came to me for a psychological release. I would remind them that by walking through the door they were consenting to give up all control to me and put themselves in my hands. I would "strip" them of their identities in order to let them experience freedom from the gendered expectations that many of them were fighting against. I would remove the pressure of having to know what to do next.

When I worked with men, my main focus was psychological torment, meaning I was invited in to tap dance on psychological soft spots. It takes a tremendous amount of empathy and psychological understanding to walk someone to the emotional edge and then see them safely back again. For an hour or two or more, I would keep these men (and less frequently, women) completely under my command.

Activities included flogging—you know, with those stereotypical leather mop-looking things; puppy play that involved clients running around like dogs, barking, and waving their little doggy tails; and foot fetish work that involved clients kissing my shoes, sometimes for hours at a time.

Messy food play (also known as sploshing) was a favorite, including one of my most entertaining clients who had a "pie in the face" fetish. Another popular activity was turning them into "human furniture." It can be difficult to be a human, but being turned into a lamp provides quite a bit more simplicity. It's actually very zen. For a predetermined amount of time, a person's only thought, only goal, only purpose in life is to keep a light shining steadily.

But these activities were never strictly sexual. They were all about creating mental experiences geared toward an emotional state of submission, based on my clients' needs. Submission is about conscientiously giving up control to a person you trust. Most of us are responsible for so many things that it can be a dramatic relief to give up the reins to someone else, to follow commands and be silly, and to express ourselves in vulnerable or theatrical ways.

On the other hand, when I coached women on how to build their confidence as the dominant partner in the bedroom, the goal was more about helping them create a different world in which they had the power and the confidence—and, sometimes most importantly, the permission—to get their needs met. We started by breaking down the beliefs that were holding them back, like the idea that "demanding" women are undesirable, or that a woman who is confident in the bedroom must be a slut (and that being a slut is a bad thing).

Being able to articulate and examine these beliefs so we could discuss them and examine how inaccurate they were, was the first step to freeing women up to understand what they wanted from their sex life going forward. We would talk through prior frustrating experiences. Discussing how those experiences affected their confidence and ability to express themselves.

Then, we started to work on embodying sexual confidence, or dominance. It's important to note here that sexual confidence—much like any confidence—comes in many forms. We would work to figure out exactly what that looked like for each individual woman. For some, it was about unleashing their sensuality and learning to move with fluidity and seductiveness. For others, it was about creating an air of superiority in order to command their partners with a cold assurance—so that not only would their needs be met, but also quickly and with enthusiasm.

We worked on tone of voice and body language. We chose "power" names that would only be used in intimate situations, and we got comfortable with the language required to clearly communicate needs, limits, and desires. I taught these women that prioritizing their desires in the bedroom would actually make them *more* attractive to their partners, because their partners wouldn't have to guess at what would make them happy.

Repeatedly, I saw women become bolder in the bedroom, and that naturally started to impact other aspects of their lives.

The journeys I guided these women on wasn't all that dissimilar from my own journey to find and embrace my unique style of confidence, both in my everyday life and in my unconventional profession. Now that we live in a post-*Fifty Shades* world, people are a little bit more familiar with kink and BDSM, but I still encounter a lot of judgment about what it means to be a dominatrix. I can't control what people think about kink or about who I am, so I've had to teach myself to simply care less about other people's opinions. It has been quite a journey.

I was raised to be a people pleaser, and that socialization was at odds with my natural personality, which has always been brash and demanding and interested in expressing my own experience in life. Being a dominatrix created a very simple filter to help me see who I needed in my life and who I did not. Early in my career I got a certain pleasure out of being a bit confrontational about my choices. So if I went to a non-kink friend's barbecue and somebody asked, "What do you do?" I'd say, "I'm a dominatrix," right away. My attitude would communicate a kind of dare to find it scandalous.

I tended to lead with that automatic defensiveness so I could get the judgment over with. I discovered that people had one of four responses to hearing that I was a dominatrix.

1. Immediate Disgust: No matter how articulate, interesting, or pleasant they may have thought I was just moments before, I suddenly became repulsive in some people's eyes. There were multiple times when people physically backed away from me, as if my career choices were contagious.

2. Ice: Some people would just freeze me out, immediately shutting themselves down and the conversation. While that could be painful, it was a gift because it allowed me to see which people were not approaching life from a place of curiosity.

3. Objectification: Others would latch on to the salaciousness of it. They were very interested in hearing more, but they stopped seeing me as a person and they started seeing me as an inaccurate, highly sexualized stereotype.

4. Curiosity: Finally, there were people whose interest came from a place of curious, non-judgmental positivity, and those were the folks who I would continue talking with and who often developed into actual friends.

These reactions gave me a clue to the way people I met viewed the world, viewed women, and viewed me. Being very forthright about my profession gave me a quick mechanism to see what type of person I was interacting with, and I've adopted that mechanism in other facets of my life—I make no apologies for who I am or how I express myself, and I can tell immediately by someone's reaction whether that person is worth continuing a conversation with.

Because more than anything, being a professional bitch allowed me to grow into my confidence in a way, that I think with any other professional environment, would have taken quite a bit longer.

My entire worldview is shaped by my experience in the kink world, and it's given me tools I apply to every important aspect of my life. Here are just a few of the lessons I've learned in the kink world, and that I hope you take away from this book:

- Boundaries are a healthy and positive thing to verbalize and share with other people.

- Communicating clearly allows me to get exactly what I want and need from people and to understand what they need from me.

- Going over the top and being the biggest, fullest version of myself can be celebrated. There are people who will love me in all of my intensity and be grateful for the traits that the rest of the world says are not okay.

- Limits are good, and liking what I like and leaving the rest for others is a beautiful, healthy thing.

- Consent is important both in and out of the bedroom.

- Confidence is expressed in a myriad of different ways, and a person's dramatic individuality is something to be curious and excited about.

Much of domination (and kink in general) is about exploring, confronting, and overturning social taboos. I found this to be a critical aspect of my own journey to let go of what others think of me, and explore the version of myself that is the strongest and most interesting to *me*. This concept and these tools have empowered me to be my full self and interact with folks of all genders in a way that focuses on communication, mutual respect, and boundaries.

In this book, I'm going to share these tools with you. But before we get into the good stuff, I want to make a few things clear, namely, what this book is and isn't about.

What This Book Is NOT

This book is not about making you do kinky things. You don't need to be kinky at all—you don't have to even know anything about kink—in order to get a lot out of my techniques. What you do need is to have an open mind to what I'm trying to do, which is to bring to a wider audience a truly effective self-improvement tool that's also fun, edgy, creative, and out-of-the-box.

This book is not about sex. The things I'll be suggesting aren't about sex at all. But I will be encouraging you to look to non-traditional experiences to gain benefits and perspectives that you may be missing otherwise.

This book is not about simply commiserating over the issue of the Bitch Stigma. I don't want to just say, "Oh, this is happening and it sucks," because women don't need to be told that it's happening: we live it every day. In casual conversations, when I say, "The Bitch Stigma," I've never had a single woman ask, "What is that?" They immediately say, "I've never heard that phrase, but I know exactly what you're talking about."

This book isn't about asking women to do more work. We're constantly having to invest effort in being more aware of other people's responses, of caring even more and prioritizing even more what other people think, and how we're being perceived.

Lean In[2] was an attempt to give women a new framework to work within. But, in the end, it was nothing new, and it was rooted in a lot of privilege. It seemed at first to be a new technique, but it just ended up being some of the same old thing, and women are tired of being told the same things.

This book isn't about man-bashing or man-hating in any way. Men have their own struggles, most of which I call the "Macho Mindset" (aka toxic masculinity) that traps them in gender stereotypes too. This is not to dismiss bad behavior or the unfortunate reality of sexism that is often both unconsciously AND willfully perpetuated.

This book is also not about encouraging women to be "bitches" in the toxic sense of the word or about asking women to change who they are. Rather, I'll be introducing a system to help women identify and embrace their own unique badass power (more on that later).

What This Book IS

This book is about really breaking out of the box and using lessons from an entirely different subculture to improve the way we live in our own skin as confident women.

In the United States at least, we are not given the tools or language to understand or explore our own sexuality, and I think the same is true for women discovering their confidence.

Because most of us are not given these tools directly, we are forced to figure it out on our own, piecing together what confidence looks like by observing confident female behavior in pop culture, movies, and the few successful women who make it to the top. As a result, we're left with both gaps of knowledge and self-doubt in a culture that doesn't readily provide support but often provides pressure to stay in our lane. Our self-doubt leads us to develop the opposite of what we're trying to achieve in the first place, which is confidence.

The goal of this book is to give women those tools and to empower us to be bold and stop shrinking in the hopes it will get us what we want and need.

I'm sharing new, actionable ways to break out of these long-held belief systems (both conscious and unconscious) and figure out ways to embody our own strengths in all aspects of our lives: in our professional lives, in our personal relationships, and in the ways that we see ourselves. If we want to make waves as women, we need to stop giving the "bitch" label any power over us.

What Are We Going to Do About It?

The truth is that being perceived as bitches can also prevent us from moving forward in our professional and personal lives. That's just how society works. I wish I could say that there was a formula to "fix" this situation, but that wouldn't be a realistic promise. However, I can give you formulas to help women share their own voices and live their lives with more integrity. After all, if we're already unhappy because catering to the world isn't getting us where we want to go, we might as well stop catering.

I don't need to tell you what the Bitch Stigma is because you're living it. I don't need to convince you that the Bitch Stigma exists because you're living it. And I don't need to tell you about the consequences of being perceived as a bitch because you've spent your entire life avoiding them. What I do need to do is give you some new and innovative tools and techniques to become even stronger than you already are.

Also, I need to do it all without taking up too much of your time, because you have a world to conquer.

This book is an action plan to help you stop diminishing yourself and start standing more firmly in your power. This book will help you EMBODY your power and to tap into the strengths and skills you already possess.

My out-of-the-box approach comes from living a life in which I've been unwilling

to flatten myself for the comfort of others. My methods come from a lifetime of helping hundreds of women let go of the myths that dictate their behavior and restrict them from fulfilling their desires.

I'll teach you how to recontextualize the "bitch" label—whatever that looks like for you, specifically—so that, if you want to, you can wear it with pride, or at the very least neutralize its negative power over you.

How Are We Going to Do That?

It starts with perspective.

Part of the solution is working from the inside out. Examining your own beliefs and finding the spots where those beliefs are creating unnecessary limitations.

Stop focusing on the perception (outside-in) and start focusing on the intention (inside-out).

Before we go any further, let me make a disclaimer: I'm not telling you to completely stop caring about anyone else's opinion. First, a truly, constantly "give no fucks" attitude sounds pathological. Second, it isn't healthy. It is important to be aware of how your actions affect others and even to care about *certain* people's opinions—that's just being a decent human. But it's equally important not to let other people's opinions stop you from doing what is right for you. You can care about others and still put yourself first. This isn't a book about totally disregarding others all the time no matter what. It's an honest, realistic, practical book to help you make the changes you need in your life to become more confident communicating your needs, setting and honoring your boundaries, and taking care of yourself—without jettisoning healthy, positive relationships.

Women are taught to cater to people's needs, to be conscious about what people think, and to behave in a way that pleases other people. The first step toward expressing yourself more confidently is shifting your perspective to let go of just about everything that you've been taught about what it means to be a strong woman.

Sure, there are tricks and techniques—power poses, catch phrases, and the like—but if you haven't managed to adjust the way you believe you deserve to exist in your life, all the power posing in the world is just that: posing. It starts with the belief that you deserve to exist as a woman, without apology and without overly policing your own behavior.

Being concerned about how others perceive us is a normal thing and we all experience it. I'm not interested in beating you up and saying you're doing it wrong. I'm not interested in changing who you are. I want to help you change the way you perceive your own actions, because your own perception is your first line of defense.

We cannot control the way that other people perceive our actions and we can't control other people's feelings no matter how much we cater to them. The belief that we can is the reason we're doing this constant tap dance of trying to get what we need done without disrupting anybody else.

Of course, focusing on our own perceptions of ourselves rather than others' perceptions is easier said than done, and throughout the book, I'm going to share some tips and tools to help you turn your focus inward and let your own needs, integrity, and authenticity drive your behavior, rather than allowing other people's needs and opinions to dictate who you are. The Mirror Matrix will help you identify and embrace your unique inner badass—whatever that looks like for you.

All of these tools will help you embrace the two major aspects to getting comfortable in our own confidence: internal perspective shifts and behavioral changes that you need to make inside of your belief systems. Both are ongoing processes, but it's important to get comfortable with the internal and external changes before you even start to think about how other people perceive you.

I'll show you several techniques for both the internal shifts and the behavior changes in this book, and we'll approach each one through several different lenses and scenarios. As a result, here are some of the main benefits I hope you'll take away:

- Increased confidence
- Less anxiety
- More resilience
- Permission from yourself to achieve your goals and dreams
- Courage to speak up for yourself
- Archetypes to recontextualize "bitchy" behavior in all its manifestations
- A life of boldness and integrity
- Higher-quality relationships
- A roadmap to realize your ambitions
- Heightened authenticity

Sounds Great, but Will It Work for Me?

For the last two decades I've been working with women and couples to improve their experiences and communication in the bedroom. The majority of my work has been helping women gain the confidence to set boundaries and demand that their needs be met.

Many of my clients found that the techniques we were working on to liberate them in the bedroom also began to liberate them in other areas of their life.

One woman I worked with was able to use the techniques I taught her to confidently ask for a raise, and she got exactly what she asked for. Another woman had a frank talk with her mother about the body-shaming language she often used around her. All of the women reported feeling more generally confident to speak up in both personal and professional settings and to set and assert boundaries in those environments.

But don't just take it from me! Here are a couple of examples of things my clients have said:

> *"You gave me one of those 'click' moments that you were talking about. Now I have some wonderful new tools to help me grow and help me negotiate to get exactly what I need out of life."*

> *"Kali taught me to embrace the dominant side of myself rather than fall into the trap of believing that being an assertive woman means being 'bitchy.' She quite literally changed my life, both in the bedroom and at work, where I've learned to stop being apologetic for having an opinion."*

The bottom line is that learning how to have difficult conversations and learning how to value yourself are skills that are useful in all areas of your life. And the bedroom is one of the most extreme places we can start to develop those skills. After all, once you learn how to ask your partner to spank you or tie you up, then asking for a raise gets all the easier.

If you read through this book and do the activities, then you'll absolutely come away with a new way of approaching confidence, communication, and boundary setting that will make you so much more powerful than you already are.

What Are You Waiting for?

"We change when the pain of staying the same is greater than the pain of changing."

—DR. JOHN TOWNSEND, AUTHOR

It's definitely time for change. Women are ready to break free from current restrictions. We're ready to speak our minds and pursue our goals regardless of how other people judge us.

Now is a prime time for the message of this book. Women are really in touch with our righteous rage on a massive scale for the first time in a long time. There are all these waves of feminism and each one is inspired by being tired of the bullshit. Women right now are experiencing two major cultural touch points that are impacting things the most: the #MeToo movement and the political discourse about women's rights to take ownership of their bodies.

There's a sense that we're being deprived of respect and bodily autonomy in a way that is more visceral than it has been since the 1960s and '70s' push for birth control. Now, fifty years later, we're having to come back to those issues again, and women are realizing how much we've actually been held back by benevolent sexism.

Sexism is pervasive. We live in a culture where it's just intrinsic to how we think about gender. But benevolent sexism is a different kind of damaging. It's a way for men and women to feel safe and to feel like there has been progress while still preserving this paternalistic approach where men care for women and handle things "for our own good." I think that we're finally seeing that benevolent sexism isn't so benevolent.

This book is a guide to busting through all of that sexist bullshit and releasing the limitations of the past. You're already an achiever and a woman who is ready to speak up and stand out. This book will help you do exactly that.

It's not going to be easy. It can be difficult to break free from old patterns, and it's scary to try something new, especially something that is known to have a backlash. Still, this *is* the time to transition away from old rules and use the incredible energy that's pulsing through us to push ourselves further into our own ambitions.

It's not as if we just suddenly figure out our self-worth and boom, we never think about it again. I still struggle with self-worth issues. I still have the occasional crippling anxiety about what other people think of me. We've been subscribing to these beliefs all our lives, and it can take a significant amount of time to learn how to undo them. Furthermore, we have to keep working even harder as our lives change. We have to keep learning how to adjust those beliefs as we evolve into new aspects of our careers or deeper aspects of our relationships.

What I'm trying to teach women runs directly counter to what we've been taught throughout our entire lives. We're literally trying to retrain our brains through exposure. The good news is, no matter how old we are, or how deeply entrenched our default behaviors are, our brains are still malleable enough to readjust if we work at it with a consistent, focused approach. That's why I'm going to talk a little bit about cognitive behavioral training in this book and how we can use frequent exposure to a new behavior as a way to change the way that we respond so it becomes reflexive. It's not easy, and it often feels easier to say, "I'll let this one go—it doesn't really matter. I'll start again next time." But, especially at first, we have to take every opportunity we get to practice our newfound perspectives and skills. When we allow small boundary crossings, it becomes that much harder to confront something that really matters, as we don't have a prior memory to draw on.

What I'm saying is that this requires practice. What better time than now to get started?

How to Use This Book

Every chapter or section will have a concept, resources, and reflective questions, and you'll also find several interactive exercises throughout the book. I'll recommend techniques to practice in no—and low—pressure situations, and I'll also encourage you to start practicing certain confidence-building phrases, even just while driving down the road.

For example, to overcome conversational bulldozers at work, I'll have you practice the phrase, "Oh, thanks. I actually wasn't quite done yet," on your own. Practicing that phrase in safe situations will give you a sense memory to draw on when you're in a much more heightened, energetic situations where you need to be more reflexive. You'll practice on your own and in low-pressure situations, and then you'll move your way up to more impactful explorations.

You could just sit down and read this book straight through. It might take you a few hours, or an afternoon, or one evening staying up late, snuggled under your covers with the light on. But, I want to encourage you to slow down and let the ideas marinate, to contemplate the ways that your life could be different and take the time to do the exercises in each section. The exercises are meant to gradually stretch your power, they're meant to challenge your current way of doing things, and they're meant to give you practice with these new tools. Give yourself time for that practice. Give yourself time for the process, and, even better, don't go through this process alone. **This is an experience**

best had with support; the support of other strong, badass women like you, who are trying to get by in a world that says, "Sit down, shut up, and smile."

Take the time, give yourself and your growth the space and energy you deserve, and recognize that when you do the work, there are rewards. The sooner you get started, the sooner you'll be living an even bigger, bolder life than you are now.

Throughout the book, I'll share journal prompts, exercises, and other activities to help you reflect on your experiences, make your plans to ditch the Bitch Stigma, and track your progress along the way. To make that easier, I've created a whole set of fun, printable worksheets and templates at BitchStigma.com/library. You can head there now and download all those fun things so they'll be ready when you are, or you can keep an eye out for a reminder of the URL throughout the book (usually next to the "Go Deeper" and "Take Action" sections), indicating that there's a template available to guide you through a reflection or exercise.

Let's get this off to a solid start by making a commitment to work through this book and make changes in your life. By putting this book into practice, you're making space to grow.

It's only when we look ahead to see the benefits of change that change becomes possible. We have to be willing to sit with the discomfort of transition and stay focused on exactly what we're going to get out of the change once we put it into practice. If we're operating on vague ideas like, "Oh I'm gonna speak up more," it quickly becomes apparent that it's just too vague, making it hard to commit consistently.

If we don't articulate the goals we're chasing after, then we'll never know if we've achieved them or not. Instead quantify them. "This is how my relationships will be different. This is how work will be different." Most importantly, "This is how I will feel about myself, my communication style, my power, and my right to take up space in the world."

Before you start reading, I want you to understand your what and your why. What do you want?

- To be more outspoken
- To set better boundaries
- To expand your existing confidence
- What else?

Why do you want to make these changes? What is going to change in your life?

In the spirit of clarifying your goals and setting your intentions, I encourage you to take a look at where you are *now* and where you'd like to be in the future.

GO DEEPER: WHERE ARE YOU NOW?

Take some time to answer the following questions:

- What are some things you do well?
- What are some things you need to work on improving?
- What is important to you? Why?
- What do you want to get out of this book/these changes?

SECTION 1

THE BITCH STIGMA

IN THIS SECTION, WE'RE GOING to dive deeper into what the Bitch Stigma is and how it affects us in our daily lives. After all, women have developed a ton of ways to work around and within the stigma. We have a system of coping mechanisms to choose from, and some of us choose to lean into the bitch stereotype while others use excessive perkiness to avoid the b-word label at all costs. To be clear, the Bitch Stigma affects different women differently depending on what I call "Bitch Privilege," and we'll look at that too. There are many characteristics other than gender—race, socioeconomic status, and sexual orientation, to name just a few—that impact the ways women cope with and combat the Bitch Stigma. All women are affected by the Bitch Stigma somehow, just to varying degrees.

We'll start with how language is used to reinforce the stigma around women being assertive and ambitious, and we'll look at the specific ways women are restricted by gendered expectations of their behavior.

Before we can implement new tools to get beyond the stigma, it helps to break it down and lay it out. Without further delay, let's get to it!

CHAPTER 1

What's in a Word?

IF YOU KNOW THE OLD playground rhyme, "Sticks and stones can break my bones, but words can never hurt me," then you also know it's a load of crap. We assign language so much weight in society, lifting others up or putting others down. When we use words as weapons, they can be incredibly harmful. In today's culture, "bitch" has become a particularly loaded word, all too often used as a weapon against women. But what if we could embrace it, taking back its power for ourselves and using it to build women up rather than tear them down?

Let's take a look at the word "bitch"—its different connotations and meanings and how, as women, we can harness its meaning to reflect and inspire our most confident selves.

What They Mean by Bitch

According to linguist and author Deborah Tannen, "*Bitch* is the most contemptible thing you can say about a woman. Save perhaps the four-letter C word."[3]

In the last few years, as I've been talking with women about the Bitch Stigma, one of the frequent questions I'm asked relates to why I've chosen the word "bitch," rather than words like "bossy" or "difficult."

Let's take a look at the other negative words that are used to describe powerful women.

Angry	Nag	Bossy
Difficult	Pushy	Shrew
Princess	Rude	Cunt
Aggressive	Shrill	Intense
Overbearing	Abrasive	Demanding
Militant	Dramatic	Intimidating
Ball-buster	Unlikable	Combative
Condescending	Unapproachable	Brusque
High maintenance	Cold/Calculating	Control freak

In recent years the *Lean In* crowd has been talking about the word "bossy," emphasizing that little girls are called bossy while little boys are taught that they're natural leaders.[4]

Characteristics that are considered manipulative in women are seen as strategic in men. Women nag, while men are persistent. Women have tunnel vision, while men exhibit visionary focus.

"Just because I have my standards, they think I'm a bitch."

— DIANA ROSS, SINGER

It's true that in business or professional settings people are much more likely to use tamer words like difficult, high maintenance, pushy, or even ball buster, but the word bitch sums up all these lesser words. Everyone's favorite research source, Wikipedia, has a pretty good definition that covers all the bases[5]:

"Bitch, literally meaning a female dog, is a pejorative slang word for a person—usually a woman—who is belligerent, unreasonable, malicious, a control freak, rudely intrusive, or aggressive. When applied to a man, bitch is a derogatory term for a subordinate [used to emasculate him]. Its original use as a vulgar term, documented from the fifteenth century, suggested high sexual desire in a woman, comparable to a dog in heat."

The word bitch is used in a specifically gendered way that's meant to cut women down, to put us back in our places, and to show disgust with any ambition or strength we might be demonstrating. It's used to indicate that a woman has gotten above herself or is asserting herself more than is considered appropriate, and it's used to show she's not being as "nice" (or "sweet" or "proper" or all-around good enough) as she should be. It's how women are referred to in rap songs to indicate how disposable and insignificant they are. When men want to denigrate other men, they frequently use the term bitch to indicate that they aren't as powerful as they should be.

While other terms like "bossy" and "difficult" carry many of the same meanings, I've chosen the more confrontational and more vulgar term: bitch. It's a word that's specifically geared toward women, and I think it's time we reclaim it.

Reclaiming the Word Bitch

"I just love bossy women. I could be around them all day. To me, bossy is not a pejorative term at all. It means somebody's passionate and engaged and ambitious and doesn't mind learning."

—AMY POEHLER, ACTRESS

The idea of language reclamation is based in power—more specifically, who has the power to define labels and decide what is negative or desirable. The word bitch is only seen as derogatory because society declares that quality to be bad, but when a word or phrase is reclaimed as a form of resistance and protest, it loses its power to be hurtful. It takes a brazen defiance for an oppressed or marginalized group (such as women) to move to redefine what was once a slur.

Adam Galinsky, an ethics professor at Northwestern University who studies reappropriation, explains that there's a difference between "claiming" a word, which excludes anyone else from using it, and reclaiming a word by flipping the meaning on its head and changing the negative stigma to a positive meaning.[6]

In the last few decades there has been an awesome surge of women reclaiming the word bitch, in the same tradition of the LGBT community reclaiming the word "queer." For example, a study published in 2013 in *Psychological Science* found that people felt more powerful after self-labeling with a derogatory term like "bitch."[7]

Here are just a few of the ways we're seeing women flip the word "bitch" on its head:

- Boss Bitch
- Basic Bitch
- You call me "bitch" like it's a bad thing
- **B**abe **I**n **T**otal **C**ontrol of **H**erself

Since the 1990s, women have been reclaiming the term bitch in pop culture, from songs like "Da Baddest Bitch" from Trina[8] to a softer interpretation by Meredith Brooks simply titled "Bitch."[9] Madonna said in a 1995 interview, "I'm tough, ambitious, and I know exactly what I want. If that makes me a bitch, OK."

In 1996, Lisa Jervis and Andi Zeisler founded *Bitch* magazine.[10]

In 1998, Elizabeth Wurtzel wrote *"Bitch: In Praise of Difficult Women"* saying, "I intend to do what I want to do and be who I want to be and answer only to myself. That is, quite simply, the bitch philosophy."[11]

By the early 2000s, the term bitch had become incredibly flexible in a way that allowed users to adapt it to their own needs and intentions. Of course, who is using the word and how it's intended impacts its meaning. For example, in a 2013 episode of *Parks and Recreation* called "Gin it Up!" there's a great exchange between Donna and Leslie about the difference between a "Bitch Boss" and a "Boss Bitch" that's an excellent example of how the word can be used in either a derogatory way or a celebratory way.[12] It's still derogatory and sexist when it's used to demean women. Calling a woman a bitch when she's demonstrating power is still a form of power dynamics.

In the kink world there's a joyful celebration of women who are "bitch goddesses"–women who don't take any shit from anyone and are celebrated for their strength and individuality. Tony Thorne, curator of the Slang and New Language archive at King's College London, calls out the use of the word as a "new ironic or comic positive usage, mainly among young females, for girl(friend)."[13] And in a fantastic TEDx talk from 2017 titled, "Why You Need to Be a Bitch," Tabatha Coffey (star of reality hairstyling show *Tabatha Takes Over*) shares her redefinition of the word bitch:[14]

Brave, **I**ntelligent, **T**enacious, **C**reative, **H**onest
Now that's an acronym I can get behind!

What I Mean by Bitch

I use the word bitch throughout this book to mean, "an empowered woman unhindered by gendered and sexist expectations."

By my definition, being a bitch is a powerful thing, though it can certainly be used to identify toxic behavior or to tear women down. The term is highly nuanced, and you'll see it used to identify both "Badass Bitches" and "Toxic Bitches" throughout the book (though I will never use it with the intent to tear women down). But, in general, for me at least, being called a bitch brings to mind the recent rallying cry of, "Nevertheless, she persisted," because that's exactly what powerful women do. We don't allow others to restrict us "bitches" for their own comfort.

As *Bitch Magazine* says on their "About Us" page: "If being an outspoken woman means being a bitch, we'll take that as a compliment."[15]

Personally, I deeply relate to this section of "The BITCH Manifesto," authored by feminist attorney Jo Freeman (Joreen) in 1968:

> *"A Bitch takes shit from no one. You may not like her, but you cannot ignore her....[Bitches] have loud voices and often use them. Bitches are not pretty....Bitches seek their identity strictly through themselves and what they do. They are subjects, not objects...Often they do dominate other people when roles are not available to them which more creatively sublimate their energies and utilize their capabilities. More often they are accused of domineering when doing what would be considered natural by a man."[16]*

For me, being a bitch is revolutionary. Refusing to allow others to demean my strength only makes me more powerful.

Of course, not everyone identifies with the word bitch, nor do all women want to reclaim it.

As I've talked with women over the years, the most frequent response to my question: "Do you self-identify as a bitch?" has been, "I'm a strong woman, but I don't identify as a bitch." This is understandable considering how the word has been used to demean women for decades.

Not everyone feels comfortable with the idea of "reclaiming" a negative word, and that's okay. There are plenty of other ways to identify and embrace your own unique strength and power. Here are just a few to consider:

Tenacious	Outspoken	Gutsy
Candid	Sincere	Fierce
Free	Bold	Fearless
Courageous	Commanding	Poised
Unapologetic	Formidable	Brilliant
Daring	Edgy	Powerful
Maverick	Memorable	Tough
Self-assured	Powerhouse	Forceful
Independent	Straight-forward	Vibrant

Later on, I'm going to introduce the Mirror Matrix, which breaks down the word "bitch" into a range of subcategories based on different ways we can show power and confidence. Why the "Mirror Matrix"? Because this system is all about shifting our focus away from how society sees us and instead paying attention to how we see ourselves. Rather than helping us fit into predefined boxes, the Mirror Matrix is meant to be a tool for self-reflection and self-centric personal development on our own terms. You may not identify as a "bitch," and that's okay. Instead, you might identify as a warrior, a rebel, an advocate, or a queen, among other things. But more on that later.

GO DEEPER: WHAT DOES THE WORD "BITCH" MEAN TO YOU?

Language is very personal, so let's stop for a minute to figure out what these words mean to you.

- Do you remember the first time you heard someone called a bitch?

- Write down all the associative words you can think of related to bitch.

- Which of these words is most triggering for you? Why do you think that is?

- What did it trigger in you? Anger, anxiety, frustration, sadness, something else?

CHAPTER 2

The Stigma: Respect Versus Likability

"We teach girls to shrink themselves. To make themselves smaller. We say to girls, 'You can have ambition, but not too much. You should aim to be successful, but not too successful.'"

—CHIMAMANDA NGOZI ADICHIE, AUTHOR

THE WORLD IS AFRAID OF powerful women, and it has been for a long time. When a woman knows she's powerful, when she stands in that power, that makes her a danger to the status quo. It's not surprising that society has developed a system for keeping women feeling powerless.

Ambitious women experience backlash to the very behaviors that are necessary to be successful, and we're penalized when we behave in ways that violate gender stereotypes.

The expectation that women should constantly be nurturing, agreeable, warm, and helpful frames any behavior perceived as outside of those norms as deviant. If a woman is high-achieving, decisive, or forceful, she's violating those norms, and that makes her "unlikable," even if her actions would be celebrated if she were a man.

"Our expectations for how a person in authority should behave are at odds with our expectations for how a woman should behave. If a woman talks in ways expected of women, she is more likely to be liked than respected. If she talks in ways expected of men, she is more likely to be respected than liked."

—DEBORAH TANNEN, *TALKING FROM 9 TO 5: WOMEN AND MEN AT WORK*[17]

Our current society is either unable or unwilling to teach women how to communicate with strength or express "unpleasant" emotions. When we express even the slightest frustration, we're labeled as angry or raging bitches, and angry women are ugly women (we're told) because rage, no matter how righteous, doesn't fit in that tiny box of ladylike behavior.

"As a man gets more successful, he is better liked by men and women, and as a woman gets more successful, she is less liked by men and women."

—SHERYL SANDBERG, *LEAN IN*[18]

It's not that there's this *one specific behavior* that will make people think we're bitches. But when the people we work with perceive us as bitches, it can seriously impact our professional relationships, interactions, and opportunities. The more powerful we appear, the more anxious they feel, and that creates a self-perpetuation spiral that doesn't do us, as powerful women, any good.

So we end up having to choose: are we going to pursue our ambition and risk being judged harshly for it, or will we choose to be likable and risk sabotaging our own progress? This catch-22 is the heart of the Bitch Stigma.

The Bitch Stigma isn't about our *actual* behavior, but about the *perception*—other people's and our own—of that behavior.

Unconscious bias and power dynamics are the two sides of a coin that creates the Bitch Stigma. Our brains automatically make quick judgements and assessments of people and situations, even when we don't intend to do so. We form judgments about people based on everything from their clothes to their names, even if we know we shouldn't, and we don't intend to. Not all bias is unconscious though, and some men and women perpetuate the Bitch Stigma because they actively want to keep the current system—which has given them power they enjoy—in place. Men depend on the Bitch Stigma to keep women behaving politely and women are often enforcers as well.

Because of this, women spend a tremendous amount of energy and effort moderating their behavior in the elusive hope of being able to control what others think of them in an attempt to overcome unconscious or willful bias.

> *"I would rather be hated for who I am*
> *than loved for who I'm not."*
>
> —KURT COBAIN, SINGER-SONGWRITER

This iconic quote is one of my own personal mottos, but it's the antithesis to the messaging that a lot of us hear as we're growing up.

The socialization of women to be polite, quiet, supportive, and pleasant starts early and comes at us from all directions. Gender roles are asserted and established through how we're allowed to play and what aspects of exploration get restricted.

"What are little boys made of?
What are little boys made of?
Snips and snails
And puppy-dogs' tails
That's what little boys are made of
What are little girls made of?
What are little girls made of?
Sugar and spice
And everything nice
That's what little girls are made of."[19]

We learn early that anything other than "sugar and spice and everything nice" will be met with annoyance, frustration, and disdain. When we act like we're made of anything else, people think poorly of us. Women and Assigned Female At Birth (AFAB) children are taught to not rock the boat, to make friends, to be team players, whereas a lot of little boys and Assigned Male At Birth (AMAB) kids are taught to be aggressive, to be winners, and to be at the top of the heap.

> *"When women use conversational strategies designed to avoid appearing boastful and to take the other person's feelings into account, they may be seen as less confident and competent than they really are."*
>
> —DEBORAH TANNEN, *TALKING FROM 9 TO 5: WOMEN AND MEN AT WORK*[20]

Women spend more time navigating other people's emotional needs than we do pursuing our own goals, and we are often gaslit about our experiences as men (and toxic or unsupportive women) undermine us and sow self-doubt by telling us that we're being too sensitive, or that they didn't mean it that way, or that we've misunderstood.

In short, it often feels like we can't win. We're damned if we do and damned if we don't. The Bitch Stigma is the social conditioning that tells us that no matter what we're doing, it's probably wrong, and it's probably gonna piss somebody off.

But it's not just others' perceptions we're battling; it's our own, long-ingrained perceptions as well. "Don't rock the boat. Don't be too harsh. Above all, don't let anyone think that you're a bitch." That's the narrative we tell ourselves, and we do it because we've been taught, directly and indirectly, that our sole purpose in life is to walk that oh-so-fine line between protecting ourselves and catering to everyone around us.

Like Goldilocks, we're constantly, desperately trying to achieve behavior that is "just right."

But the reality is that there is no Goldilocks bed that prevents people from thinking their own thoughts about us, or perceiving us through the filters of their own lives and perceptions. There are ways to manage some of it, but the most important place to turn if we want to start letting go of the Bitch Stigma is inside of ourselves

Coping Mechanisms

In an attempt to minimize the number of people we piss off just by existing and being our bold, badass selves, we've developed a whole selection of ways to manage how others perceive us. Women learn to be adaptable, and we tend to either soften or harden ourselves depending on which tactic seems like it will be best received.

Let's take a look at some of the techniques women use to avoid the Bitch Stigma.

HYPER FEMININE PRESENTATION

I host in-person events for women looking to ditch the Bitch Stigma, including regular meetups, workshops, and retreats. One of the techniques many of the women in my groups use is to make their presentation hyper feminine to counteract the hardness of their communication styles and content. Rather than using soft language (which we'll discuss in detail later on), they're making themselves more "palatable" through soft presentation. This allows men and other people to accept their nontraditional confidence because it's coming from a traditional package.

Hyper feminine presentation generally refers to the way we dress and make ourselves up. Multiple women in my group have talked about wearing dresses and soft colors, keeping our hair long and flowing, and using makeup to round out a "correct" feminine appearance. They've shared how the "softness" of their appearance has made it easier for them to communicate more assertively because they're adhering to other gender norms.

UPTALK & VOCAL FRY

As women, we often adopt certain vocal patterns—often subconsciously—as another way to make ourselves appear either more or less intimidating depending on which we feel a situation calls for. Two common ones are vocal fry and uptalk.

Vocal fry is a low, creaky vibration produced by the fluttering of the vocal cords. (Think Kim Kardashian—and if you're not familiar with her, search YouTube for clips of her speaking, or even just for "vocal fry." You'll see what I mean.) Physically, we achieve vocal fry by artificially lowering the pitch of our voices, which changes the way our vocal cords vibrate and has the side effect of making us sound a little froggy. The subconscious intent here is to lower our pitches to imitate more respected groups—men and older women—and borrow some of their authority.

Uptalk, on the other hand, is an upward inflection that makes everything we say sound like a question. (Think of the traditional Valley Girl voice.) Rather than sounding decisive, we sound tentative and approval seeking, which undermines our authority. When we use this as a coping mechanism, it's to soften assertive language by making it sound less powerful.

But unfortunately, research has found that these coping mechanisms are more likely to backfire. According to a study out of Duke University, "Relative to a normal speaking voice, young adult female voices exhibiting vocal fry are perceived as less competent, less educated, less trustworthy, less attractive, and less hirable."[21] Uptalk has similar effects. Both patterns can negatively impact work relationships because of the harsh way women who exhibit them are judged, particularly by middle-aged white males. It's another damned if you do, damned if you don't situation.

If you find yourself using uptalk or vocal fry to avoid sounding "bitchy," remember that your real power is in your natural voice. If your natural speaking voice includes vocal fry or uptalk, it's time to let go of your worry. It's sexist and biased when someone judges you based on the tone of your voice, so their opinion can go right in the trash.

EXCESSIVE PERKINESS (OR, SMILEY FACE EXCLAMATION POINT DISEASE)

Another common coping mechanism is making ourselves come across as excessively perky in order to sound less blunt and off-putting. For example, have you ever caught yourself using a lot of exclamation points and smiley faces in written communication? This is one of my personal coping mechanisms, because I often fear that I'm coming across as stern or pissed off when I'm just trying to be direct or matter-of-fact. In person, I counteract that with exaggerated perkiness, complete with resting nice face no matter how I really feel. In writing, that perkiness takes the form of excessive exclamation points and smiley faces as I try to convey that "I'm happy! :) This is pleasant! :P You like me! :D." Usually I have to go back through e-mails and delete two thirds of the exclamation points while physically restraining myself from replacing them with smiley faces.

I unconsciously learned pretty early in my life that if I sounded like a cheerleader, my bluntness would be easier for folks to receive, and it's a constant battle to counteract that programming.

EMOTIONAL STOICISM

The opposite of all the perkiness is stoicism. To fight the stereotype that all women are hysterical and driven by their emotions (as opposed to men, who are generally assumed to be driven by logic), some women learn to put on an unemotional face and a kind of stoicism as armor.

This technique is often employed in corporate environments by women who spend a lot of time surrounded by men and need to seem unflappable to gain respect or maintain authority. (Of course, if you'll recall many of the criticisms against Hillary

Clinton in the 2016 presidential election, you'll notice that, in avoiding the appearance of being "hysterical," we often wind up being called "robots" or "ice queens.")

LEANING INTO THE BITCH PERCEPTION (AKA BEING 'HARD')

The opposite side of excessive perkiness is leaning into the bitch perception. This is the "I'll reject you before you reject me" mode, and it refers to the woman who constantly asserts that she "gives no fucks" or "has no more fucks to give." These women lean hard into the bitch persona, fully embracing it on their own rather than letting anyone foist it on them.

All Outta Nice—When Coping Mechanisms Fail

"Hey pretty lady, you should smile!"

Resting bitch face (also known as RBF) is the slang term that has become popularized since a viral video in 2013 introduced the concept.[22] It describes women who don't naturally present with perky smiles, and it has everything to do with policing the way women present ourselves.

We're always supposed to be wrapped in softness and sugar and spice and to be pleasant and polite and delightful. While the particulars of how we're supposed to present may vary based on our particular cultures or families or those kinds of things, as a broad social expectation, we ask women to be happy and to perform happiness for other people.

When a woman doesn't have a smile plastered on her face—often because she just doesn't have the energy to perform any-more—she falls into what has become known as "resting bitch face." It started as a derogatory term, and people still use it that way, but it's been amazing to see how women have reclaimed the phrase lately. One of my favorite recent memes is, "You should see my *active* bitch face." Collectively, we're starting to reinforce the idea that it's not our responsibility to perform happiness for other people.

But still, resting bitch face is a highly gendered, negative concept, and science has shown that women are judged harshly for this imagined contempt.

In a project titled "Throwing Shade: The Science of Resting B*tch Face," behavioral researchers Abbe Macbeth and Jason Rogers used artificial intelligence software called Face-Reader, which indexes more than 10,000 facial expressions, to study perceptions of women's neutral expressions.[23] Facereader found that there was a small amount of contempt being identified in women's resting faces, even when the expressions didn't reflect true contempt. You can even test to see if you have RBF at TestRBF.com![24]

The flip side, as I've mentioned, is to use "Resting Nice Face": putting on a happy face no matter how you feel. After all, how can people think you're a bitch if you're smiling? But actively disconnecting our facial expression from our emotional state can be damaging, too, as we're liable to be perceived as "fake" or inauthentic.

And resting bitch face isn't just about our facial expressions. "Resting bitch tone" refers to the way our voices sound when we don't take care to inject any extra perkiness. When I put my excessive perkiness coping mechanism away, people tend to think I'm a judgy bitch because I'm not using sugary tones and soft language. But, like resting bitch face, resting bitch tone is not about being rude. It's about speaking directly without concerning ourselves with how other folks might possibly be experiencing our tone. In the same way that resting bitch face is all about not putting on a sunny, smiling face for the world, resting bitch tone is about not putting a sugary sweet note to our voices.

Of course, my resting bitch tone is probably partly natural and partly attributable to spending years being paid exorbitant amounts of money to speak in withering tones to whimpering men.

"Being yourself can be a revolutionary act. And in a world that wants us to whisper, I choose to yell."

—Luvvie, TED talk[25]

Should Women Act Like Men?

At one of my Bitch Stigma meetups we were talking about how typically gendered communication styles can be a "damned if you do, damned if you don't" situation for women. When women communicate in ways that are typically considered masculine—when we're very straightforward or we swear, or we decline to use any softening or apologetic language—it comes across very differently than when those same styles are used by men.

We're not judged by the same communication standards as men, so when we communicate like men, both men and women tend to find us off-putting. It really isn't simply a matter of, "Oh, if women act like men, then they are treated the way that men are," because that's not the case.

A woman gets labeled arrogant, while a man who exhibits the same behavior gets labeled confident, direct, or a go-getter. He doesn't waste time, he's no-nonsense. He's a leader. He's an innovator. She's demanding. He's brimming with ideas. She's too opinionated.

On the flip side, if women embody "women's behaviors," then we are looked down on for being too soft.

We are expected to understand when to be polite and friendly and compassionate and nurturing, and to know exactly when and how to get just the right amount of more direct so that we can be heard without offending anyone. That's how we're supposed to say no as women, and these stories that are coming out in the #MeToo movement are demonstrating how this socialization of women to be unfailingly polite is backfiring on everyone.

It's worth noting that the socialization men receive can be equally damaging, and toxic masculinity is very real in our society as well. I want to be clear that I'm not saying all men have it super easy all the time, and I'm not encouraging universal man-hating in this book. It's just that this particular project isn't about them or their needs.

"Both women and men pay a price if they do not behave in ways expected of their gender: Men who are not very aggressive are called "wimps," whereas women who are not very aggressive are called "feminine." Men who are aggressive are called "go-getters," though if they go too far, from the point of view of the viewer, they may be called "arrogant." This can hurt them, but not nearly as much as the innumerable labels for women who are thought to be too aggressive—starting with the most hurtful one: bitch."

—DEBORAH TANNEN, AUTHOR OF *TALKING FROM 9 TO 5: WOMEN AND MEN AT WORK*[26]

GO DEEPER: HOW IS THE BITCH STIGMA IMPACTING YOU?

- What coping mechanisms do you use to avoid the Bitch Stigma in your professional or personal interactions?

- Have you ever been told that you have Resting Bitch Face or Resting Bitch Tone? If so, what do you say to people who call you out for it?

- How has the Bitch Stigma impacted the way you interact with the world? What have you learned about the expectations of your behavior?

TAKE ACTION: DEFINE YOUR RELATIONSHIP TO THE BITCH STIGMA

- Across the top of a piece of paper, write the following in order to create columns: Work, Family, Friends, Romantic Partners, and Safety. You may need multiple sheets of paper to give yourself plenty of room. (Alternatively, you can download my premade template!)

- Set a timer to write for 20 minutes and list every example or situation you can think of under each column in which the Bitch Stigma is preventing you from communicating with strength or reaching your goals.

- Now choose one of the most impactful experiences and write down a time when the fear of being labeled/ called a bitch (or some variation of that) stopped you from doing/saying something you needed to do/say.

- On the other side of the paper, write how you would've handled the situation if you weren't being impacted by the Bitch Stigma. How would you communicate differently? How would you have handled it differently? What do you think the response would've been if you'd handled it that way?

CHAPTER 3

Recognizing Risk

LET'S BE CRYSTAL CLEAR HERE: the Bitch Stigma is *very* real and can definitely have consequences. So, it's important that you discern how and when it's a good time for you to assert yourself. It's important that you keep yourself safe.

Staying Safe

I'm someone who tends to confront sexism and racism on the spot. If you say something that I think is sexist or racist, I'm going to call you out on it. But, the context of the situation matters. For example, one day my car broke down, and I had to call a tow truck. I was riding in the passenger seat, trapped in the tow truck vehicle with the driver when he went off on a very sexist and racist tirade about how people of certain genders and ethnicities are shitty drivers. It took everything I had to keep my mouth shut, but because my safety was a factor—after all, this guy was bigger than me, stronger than me, and in charge of the very small space we were both trapped in—I didn't argue. It's important to acknowledge that standing up for yourself is part of the solution, but you always need to prioritize your safety first. There are times when it is not appropriate or safe to speak up. We still live in a world that is not going to always receive that.

Speaking up on the internet can also present safety concerns. Look at everything that's happening with women being doxxed—meaning their private contact information is posted online with the intent of harmful exposure. That's not something I currently have an answer to. I speak up most of the time in person and address this stuff head on, but I don't express all of my opinions online. I love Twitter. I use Twitter daily. I think Twitter can be amazing if you use it as a connection and information tool. But, I am more careful about the things that I tweet because I know I'm sharing my thoughts with a whole world of misogynists on that platform. I'm better at speaking up in person where I can gauge the threat level directly.

There are times when we need to be badasses and speak up. Then there are times when we need to prioritize our safety and not take responsibility for every moment in the world. While change requires consistency and a certain level of risk, it's not just a light switch where you go from not speaking up to speaking up every single time, the situation be damned.

Often, those debates over speaking up or staying safe arise most often when we're dealing with men in the world. When a romantic partner says something sexist, it's probably fine (and smart) to take him to school. But when we're walking home late at night and find ourselves being followed or harassed, the objective shouldn't be to educate the guy, but to get to a safe place.

If speaking up will mean losing your job, you need to weigh the risks. If you have other options on the table, that's one thing. But if losing that job will put you in a situation that is detrimental to your health and well being, then *you do not need to feel guilty for staying quiet.* Sometimes it's physically dangerous to speak up. Or you might have a very reasonable belief that you won't be believed or that speaking up will undermine all of your other achievements. It's about finding ways that work for you, and in many cases that means finding a way to ensure the harassment doesn't continue *without* putting your reputation or your safety at risk.

The Bitch Stigma can impact every aspect of your life, but that doesn't mean you have to tackle all those areas at once. Success is easiest when it can build on itself. You're more likely to build enduring strength of habits by starting with something that's actually manageable and building confidence, and then expanding the techniques into more challenging, precarious situations in your life.

It's Not Just Men

When I launched the first Bitch Stigma Meetup group, I'll admit my own bias was that I thought we would be talking a lot about how men create obstacles for women.[27] But in fact, a lot of the women talked about how other women in their workplace are, at times, their biggest hindrance. It turns out that women in the workplace are a special obstacle all their own. Rather than being collaborators and supporters, some women can be backstabbing underminers.

Women can be affected by what I call "Queen of the Mountain Syndrome." We'll get into that more later, but in short, it comes from the belief that there's only room for one at the top. That's true for marginalized folks in general: whether it's about race or gender or any sort of marginalized identity, there are often only one or two seats at the table for those folks. That's tokenism: a symbolic or superficial effort that gives the appearance of equality without any substantive changes or initiatives.

A lot of women have had this "Queen of the Mountain" experience. Queens of the mountain can be any age or stage in life, but they're often women of an older generation who've had to fight and claw and step on anyone and everyone to get to where they are. Then they end up keeping other women down because they're afraid of losing that status and of losing their very limited space at the table. It's understandable, but that doesn't make it any less unfortunate.

When it comes to overcoming the Bitch Stigma, our obstacles are not just the men.

WRAP-UP

The change starts with you, but that's just the beginning.

A lot of women's empowerment books take a rah-rah approach that says that all you must do is think good thoughts, and even if you're the only one making a change, you'll transform your life.

I'm a realist, so I take a different approach. I firmly believe that no systemic change can happen without individual change, but it's critical to remember that's not the *only* thing that matters. We still live in a world that discourages (or is outright hostile to) women speaking up and setting clear boundaries. Some folks we interact with are willfully obtuse, some are afraid of what your growth means for them, and some will end up being a wall for no real apparent reason.

This is not meant to discourage you, but it is intended to create space for experiences that don't suddenly flip to the new paradigm. It's entirely possible to speak clearly and confidently and still be misunderstood. Whether it's in personal relationships or in professional interactions, there's a strong chance you're going to do everything right, and things still may not go your way.

But this is how revolution happens. In tiny ripples that grow into waves and accumulate to become a roaring tide. We'll talk throughout this book about ways to set yourself up to feel successful even if the outcome of specific circumstances don't go exactly to plan.

SECTION 2
THE BITCH SPECTRUM

PEOPLE OFTEN THINK THAT BITCHES are just mean, rude people. Certainly, that's true for toxic bitches. But for good bitches (aka badasses), that's not the case.

There's a *huge* difference between a woman who is confident and one who is arrogant. Yet they're often lumped in together.

Bold badass behavior includes setting boundaries, believing in your own authority, and expecting to be respected. Toxic bitch behavior includes being catty, condescending, and backstabbing. Those are traits we're obviously not trying to cultivate or perpetuate.

When I say we need to embrace the bitch, that doesn't mean we need to go too far in the other direction and stop caring at all about how we communicate or behave affects other people. I'm saying we need to find a middle ground where we can be kind without always being nice. We can stop softening, buffering and apologizing without offending. We can care about how others receive our communication without taking responsibility for their emotional experiences.

CHAPTER 4

Bitch Privilege and Intersectionality

NOT ALL WOMEN ARE TREATED equally. There are a lot of factors that impact how our behavior is received and perceived.

The Bitch Stigma is rooted in gender, but there are always additional layers to it based on whatever is most obvious about our personal presentations. Not just how we personally identify, but how *other people* see us.

These intersectional identities create extra layers of obstacles for women fighting to overcome biases outside of gender.

Bitch Privilege is created from the intersectional identities that affect how other people perceive our assertiveness. Everybody has a varied list of intersectional identities. I'm a white, cisgender, straight appearing, middle class, thin woman, and so that that gives me a certain extra allowance to be louder, bitchier, and more aggressive in social situations. I have a lot of bitch privilege. In other words, I'm going to have a lot of room to assert my power before I risk being called a bitch. None of these characteristics have anything to do with my actual behavior or its rightness or wrongness. But they do dictate the way people will perceive me and respond to me based on their own filters and biases.

Intersectionality

One of the first things I prioritized when I decided to write this book was that I wanted to be more than just another middle-class, white, American, cisgendered woman saying, "Here are techniques that have worked for me. Therefore, they're going to work for all women."

Intersectionality (also known as intersectional feminism) is a term that was coined by Black feminist scholar Kimberlé Williams Crenshaw in 1989 to describe how different types of structural discrimination and oppression—specifically race and gender—interact and compound.[28] Its common usage has expanded to include other aspects of disadvantages such as disability, age, class, sexual orientation, gender identity, and other identity markers.

As a white, cisgendered, middle class, educated woman, it's so important to me to talk about that intersectionality. When I'm out in the world, someone might think I'm a bitch, but that doesn't carry the same sort of racial overtones or consequences that it can for women of color, who become "angry Black women" or "feisty Latinx women," and face the sexualization that can happen around anger or boundary setting. For these women, "No" is often met with, "Ooo, yeah, tell me no again. That's so hot," which can feed into some pretty disgusting stuff.

I can speak from my experience, and I can provide space to talk about things that I don't have direct experience with.

Obviously, I don't have answers about being a woman of color in America. That's not something that I can speak to myself, but it's an important aspect of this conversation, and I want to make space for experiences other than my own. Intersectionality is impacting how people are perceiving them, and white women can unintentionally (and intentionally) gaslight women of color about it.

Bitch Privilege has a lot to do with acknowledging how these different factors can impact the ways that our behavior is perceived and received. They all get tallied up in people's heads to determine how much room for bitchiness any woman is allowed. As a white woman, my emotion usually gets translated simply as excitement, because white privilege allows people to ascribe positive intent to my actions. If you're a Black woman, it doesn't matter how softly you speak, because people are going to have different assumptions and biases.

When you add other marginalized identity markers to being a woman, the road to being called a bitch becomes shorter and shorter.

There's no guaranteed path through the matrix, either. It shifts according to the cultural beliefs and experiences of the people you're talking to. That's just another reminder of why we all need to let go of our fear of the Bitch Stigma. There is literally no single way we can present ourselves to avoid being labeled bitches.

It's important to note that there are several identities that can compound the bias against women.

- Age
- Race and Ethnicity
- Parenthood
- Gender presentation

- Perceived sexual orientation

- Being transgender or nonbinary

- Body type

- Beauty standards and conventional attractiveness

- Class/Financial status

- Education level

- Job title/Seniority

- Perceived sexual promiscuity/Prudishness

- English as a second language

- Shy/Outgoing

- Disability

- Religion

- Neurodivergency

Let's look at ageism as an example.

Young women are loud, snarky, perky bitches, but they have a little bit more wiggle room because there's an assumption that "that's just youth." But as women get older, that same kind of bitchiness becomes associated with bitterness and age.

And on the flip side, young women who try to assert their authority are often perceived as arrogant bitches, because people wonder what gives them the right to think they know things. As we get a little older, we have a little more room to be authoritative. Until, of course, we take our authority "too far." Many of my older women friends talk about how the perception of their authority has swung in a negative direction, so they're just written off—by their kids or anyone else they try to assert authority over—as nags or matronly bitches. The only other alternative is to become invisible and more or less fade into the background.

Privilege and Allyship

Privilege is a word that's coming up a lot in conversations and discussions these days, but not everyone knows what it really means.

Privilege refers to rights or advantages that most people don't have. In the case of "bitch privilege," these rights and advantages are generally based on characteristics outside of your control, including race, socioeconomic class, and sexuality, for starters.

With the rights and advantages of privilege come responsibility. The responsibility to be an ally, or a supporter, for others. The three first steps to being a good ally are: awareness, acknowledgement, and self-improvement. Those are the critical components to getting outside of our own perspective and of starting to move past privilege.

It is important for anyone with privilege, whether that be male privilege or straight privilege or cis privilege or white privilege or any other privilege, to take a look at how their lives have been impacted by that privilege and to understand, as well as to see, how those things have been institutionalized.

The first steps, awareness and acknowledgment, are often the hardest. When somebody points out our privilege, we often feel attacked. It's easy to go on the defensive when someone says something like, "Oh, that's your privilege talking." But here's the reality: when someone points out our privilege in a way that's intended to be constructive and helpful, that doesn't mean they're calling us a bad person. Instead, they're trying to make us aware of something so we can respond or behave accordingly. You know how it feels when someone points out that you have spinach in your teeth? It may not feel great, but it gives you a chance to improve and fix it. Think of privilege as a piece of existential spinach. We may be embarrassed, and that's okay, but we need to treat the callout as an opening to dialogue and improvement.

But it doesn't stop there. Being an ally is not an identity. It's an action. It's a verb. It's something to do. Not something to be.

We all have privilege somewhere, and privilege must speak to privilege.

I'm a huge believer that it's the responsibility of the privileged to help those who are less privileged. This isn't to say cisgendered white people need to step in and fix everything with their privilege and power. It's not about saving "damsels in distress," and it's certainly not about being a "savior." That attitude can be patronizing and counterproductive. Instead, it's about being aware of our privilege—whatever it is—and using it to stay out of the way, lift others up, and call each other out on our shit.

For example, men need to be calling out other men on their privilege or bias. When we call it out ourselves (and we should—don't get me wrong), it's too easy for men to label us as hysterical or sensitive, or write us off for "playing the gender card." We need to have men become part of the fight against sexism if we ever want anything to change, because as of now men's words often carry more weight, especially (but not solely) with other men.

The same is true for other privilege.

Look, privilege is hard to talk about. I get it. It's uncomfortable. It's awkward. We don't have the language. We don't know what is appropriate and what's not. We don't even know how to structure sentences sometimes. We're afraid to mess up.

Race and sex and gender and all the other privilege markers are things that we aren't automatically taught how to talk about in the world. These are difficult conversations and I understand that, but I also know that culture can change and that it's possible to shift thinking around difficult conversations.

How do I know that? Because for decades I've existed in a subculture that has turned conversations about the most intimate and taboo interests and experiences into the kind of straightforward, confident discussions you might have at the dinner table.

Kinksters talk about all kinds of really challenging things, but because we have a structure and because we have a language, we're at least able to grope our way (consensually of course) toward productive conversations that help us better understand each other, ourselves, and how to relate to one another. So yes, privilege is tough to talk about, but we can do it. We just need to start shifting the way we think about "difficult conversations."

GO DEEPER: HOW DOES YOUR IDENTITY IMPACT YOUR BEHAVIOR?

- What influence does your background play in your communication style and your ability to set boundaries or otherwise put yourself first?

- How does your personality come into play?

- Use the identity list on page 59 and write about how any of the identities you possess have affected the way others perceive your behavior. Have they led to privilege or marginalization? How has that impacted your ability to assert yourself? What about identities you don't possess? How might they impact your friends, relatives, or colleagues?

CHAPTER 5

The Bitch Spectrum

WE'VE SEEN OVER AND OVER again that there's a wide spectrum of behaviors that are likely to get women labeled bitches. This is what I call the Bitch Spectrum. In this section we're going to take a tour through the spectrum, starting with toxic bitches and working all the way through bold badasses.

But before we dig into all the ways we can embrace and broadcast our inner badass, let's take another look at some of the mentalities and expectations of our own and others' that power the Bitch Stigma—specifically, the deeply entrenched and utterly impossible desire so many of us have to behave "just right."

Goldilocks Syndrome (Not Too Hard, Not Too Soft)

We all know the story of Goldilocks, a little girl who finds herself in a strange house in the woods. She tastes the porridge on the table and declares each bowl either too hot or too cold. She lies in the three beds and declares each too hard or too soft, until she finds one that's "just right" and falls asleep.

Well, it turns out we all have a little Goldilocks in us. In October 2013, entrepreneur Sarah Ware wrote an article for Forbes describing what she called the "Goldilocks Syndrome," which describes women's constant quest for the perfect porridge (aka behavior) that's "just right."[29]

If you're quiet or unemotional or don't give those around you enough coddling, then you'll likely be labeled cold and you'll be avoided. If you are warm and open and eager to take care of others, you'll be labelled overbearing and you'll be avoided.

If you're assertive and opinionated, you'll likely be labeled hot and be avoided. If you shy away from sharing opinions, you'll be labeled dumb and be avoided.

See where I'm going?

All of it comes down to society's insistence on policing women's behavior and keeping us wondering how we can be perceived as "just right." We're constantly expected to walk this line of being not too hard and not too soft. If you're too hard, you get labeled a bitch. If you're too soft, you get steamrolled and overlooked. It's a constant attempt to be vigilant and navigate all of these open expectations and unstated expectations. Are you noticing that no matter how we women behave, we're screwed? There is no perfect behavior.

SELFISH BITCHES

Take self-care, for example.

Being labeled as selfish is an excellent example of how women are rarely able to be "quite right" in their behavior. Often, women who don't put others first every waking moment are written off as selfish. But really, aren't we all a little selfish?

And aren't we entitled to put ourselves first? When society tells women over and over to care for others above ourselves, then "selfishness" becomes a radical act.

The idea that self-care is not selfish is a really important modern concept. After all, there's a reason flight attendants insist you put on your own air mask before you can help others with theirs.

Selfishness is not inherently bad, but that doesn't mean that it's *always* good either. Selfishness *without self-awareness or empathy* is what causes problems. But that's because anything without self-awareness has a lot more jagged edges. In all the ways we embrace our inner bitches—from selfishness to assertiveness at work and beyond—self-awareness is the key to staying on the right side of the line between bold badass and toxic bitch.

My previous career has given me a unique perspective on selfishness because, in some ways, I made a career out of being selfish. It was my literal job to believe and act as though I was the center of the universe. (And I did. And I do.) Women are not taught to embrace that kind of egoism or selfishness. But the ironic thing is, the more intentionally selfish we are, and the more we're willing to put our foot down and put ourselves first, the better equipped we'll be to do what's expected of us, which is to take care of others.

Why Are Women Labeled Bitches?

During my workshops, I ask the question, "When and why are women labeled as bitches?" These are some of the responses I hear:

The other person feels that we are taking their power away

- When we tell somebody what to do, even if it's our literal job to tell that person what to do
- When we talk too much

- When we voice our opinions

- When we ask questions and people automatically assume we're challenging authority

- When we challenge anyone, even if we merely express an opinion contrary to theirs

- When we tell someone they're wrong—or worse, prove it

- When we don't use qualifiers like "sorry" or "I'm just…" or "maybe" to soften our messages

- When we just say no, as a full and complete sentence, with no modifiers or caveats

- And every single instance applies wherever we are— from the boardroom to the bedroom to the sidewalk.

Assailants and others will call us bitches in order to make us feel guilty and force us to back down. This could happen with a stranger in a public space or with a colleague, friend, or partner in an interpersonal argument. These people are trying to guilt us for being strong and play on our socialized instinct to be perceived as polite and good. They're positioning us as the perpetrators to stop us from enforcing our boundaries.

Here are just a few examples of the times that I have personally been called a bitch:

- When I haven't hugged someone upon greeting or saying goodbye

- When I haven't smiled the entire time that we were talking

- When I haven't invited someone into my personal space such as my home or into personal situations such as nights out with close friends

- When I have set or enforced my boundaries
- When I have expected my expertise or opinion to be respected
- When I have expected my physical boundaries to be respected
- When I have made my own sexual choices (particularly when those sexual choices have not been considered in line with the expectations of me as a woman in the world)
- When I haven't been nice enough
- When I've been too nice and someone's perceived it as fake
- When I've known too much
- When I have not known enough
- When I haven't given undeserved reassurance to the other person
- When I've told the truth and it made other people uncomfortable

Let me be clear: in none of these situations was I acting in a toxic way. It's all about the way others see these actions. If I'm asserting myself softly and politely, but I'm still asserting myself, I'm liable to be called a bitch because that's how my audience *perceives* my behavior.

Every behavior can motivate someone to call us bitches.

Here's an example: People think I'm a bitch because I talk a lot. I don't wait for someone to ask my opinion. If I have something to say, I say it. That "mouthiness" often gets me labeled a bitch. There is a woman in my Meetup group who is really shy, but people think her quietness is stuck-up disinterest and so, you guessed it, they label her a bitch.

It's a total catch-22.

Even accepting compliments can be seen as a sign of being a bitch. For example in the movie *Mean Girls*, when one young woman says, "You're pretty," and Lindsay Lohan simply says, "Thank you," she gets called out for it. The bully says, "So you agree? You think you're pretty?"[30] As if it's a bad thing for her to both accept the compliment and to think of herself as pretty.

That's one of the most dangerous things about the Bitch Stigma: Any behavior can be twisted into a derogatory accusation about a woman. In short, anytime we are not simply catering to everyone around us at all costs, that's when the Bitch Stigma strikes.

There is no perfect behavior that will allow us to escape the potential of being called a bitch. So let's stop making it our first priority to avoid being called a one.

GO DEEPER: WHAT'S IT LIKE TO BE CALLED A BITCH?

- Have you ever been called a bitch (or one of the derivative words)? What caused it?

- Which of your innate behaviors or actions are most often construed as bitchiness? How does that feel?

- Describe a time when you worked hard to find that "just right" Goldilocks sweet spot. Were you successful? What were the ramifications?

Introducing the Mirror Matrix

One of the main messages I've taught women for years in the kink space is that erotic dominance can take many styles and forms. So many women start out by thinking that dominance always has to look like an angry, leather-clad woman showing nothing but disdain for her partner. But that's just one archetype to explore and only if it's attractive to you. In fact, there are so many other styles—The Nurturer, The Classy Lady, The Brat, The Traditionalist, The Provocateur, The Girl-Next-Door, The Amazon, The Siren, and many others that may be more suitable, and therefore much more fun.

If you consider yourself someone who isn't very confident or isn't ready to embrace being a bitch, this concept is true for you too. Not all confidence needs to look the same either. All you have to do is replace the word *domination* with *confidence,* and the same message I've been teaching to kinksters for nearly two decades becomes applicable to any woman, anywhere.

I've created a system of archetypes that I call the Mirror Matrix to help you recognize the different ways confidence presents itself and to differentiate between toxic and healthy bitch behavior. The Mirror Matrix includes the full spectrum of attitudes—both Toxic Bitches who exhibit negative, undesirable behaviors and Bold Badasses who are confident and independent women. No matter where you fall on any given day or in any given situation, it's all about how *you* see yourself in the mirror.

BITCHES IN POP CULTURE, LITERATURE AND HISTORY

"I'm tough, I'm ambitious, and I know exactly what I want. If that makes me a bitch, okay."

—MADONNA, SINGER-SONGWRITER

We see a wide variety of these bitch archetypes represented in popular culture, and the way celebrity "bitches" past and present are treated greatly impacts and reinforces the way we perceive women. Thanks to books, movies, and tv shows, we have a fairly wide range of powerful women to look at to see how stereotypes are used as character shortcuts. We'll take a closer look at these archetypes and how they play out in real life shortly, but for now, here's a quick overview of some of the ways celebrity "bitches" are accepted—or not—by mainstream media and society.

Not every woman is seen as a bitch even if they've managed to achieve a high level of social power. Two of the most popular daytime hosts, Ellen DeGeneres and Oprah, are excellent examples of this. Both women have amassed an incredible amount of social clout and financial power, but they have managed to avoid the general classification of "bitch" that clouds many powerful women's reputations. These women are still seen as "likable," despite their power. I, for one, would call Ellen a Rebel and Oprah a Boss, and you can be damn sure I mean both as compliments.

Then we look at examples of women in pop culture who have actively embraced an identity as a "bitch," like Madonna or Nicki Minaj. These women are both celebrated and denigrated for living without self-imposed limitations.

Finally, there are the powerful women who find themselves written off as bitches because of the very traits that make them confident, competent, and powerful. We see this one a lot in politicians, from Hillary Clinton to Theresa May and Alexandrea Ocasio-Cortez, as people on both sides of the aisle overlook their ideologies and qualifications and focus solely on their "character flaws."

How to Use the Mirror Matrix

The Mirror Matrix is meant as a guide, to give you a tool along with language you can use to differentiate between Toxic and

Bold behavior—and to help you get acquainted with your own self-perception.

There are nine archetypes total, including three Toxic Bitches and six Bold Badasses. The grid introduces you to each archetype on its own spectrum of intensity.

Bold Badasses

Toxic Bitches

ADVOCATE

polite / tactful / formal
principled
honest / straightforward
firm
academic

WARRIOR

fierce
tireless
vigilant
passionate
intense conviction

FANATIC

opinion tornado
relentless
unmovable
aggressive / volatile
demanding
militant

QUEEN

enigmatic
dignified
aloof / remote
self-contained
woman of few words

BOSS

competent / skillful
in charge
hierarchical
collaborative
brusque / no nonsense
enforces protocols

STEAMROLLER

doesn't listen
condescending
overbearing
superior
competitive
micro-manager
oblivious

REBEL

bold
blunt
self-possessed
trailblazer
charming / influential
rebellious

ROGUE

unorthodox
radical
edgy
sharp-tongued / snarky
truth-teller
anti-establishment

TYRANT

rude / catty
arrogant
manipulative
tempermental
secretive
uses humiliation

Looking into the Mirror

You'll notice the first two columns include Bold Badasses, and the third includes Toxic Bitches. Several factors go into determining whether someone is being toxic or bold, so how can you tell the difference in your own "bitchy" behavior? All it takes is a little self-reflection.

Intention: Intention *does* matter, especially when others are likely to view our actions through the lens of the Bitch Stigma and general sexist stereotypes. So take a look at what you're trying to do and whether your intention lines up with your integrity. Most of us know when we're being toxic, even if we won't admit it out loud. Here are some questions you can ask yourself:

- What are you attempting to accomplish? What are you trying to communicate?

- Are your actions in line with your intentions?

- Are you lashing out about something that has made you angry, frustrated, disappointed, annoyed, jealous, or something else?

- Does the person you're communicating with potentially have some conscious or unconscious biases that are influencing their perception?

Impact: You can't stop at intention, though, because impact may matter too, depending on the situation. Especially if you feel conflict brewing with someone important in your life, then your intention can be overwhelmed by your impact. We'll go deeper into this in a later chapter, but you can start with these questions:

- Are your actions or behavior actually harmful to the other person?

- Does the person have a double standard for behavior they allow from other people, especially men?

- Who is this person in your life? Does their opinion matter? Why?

REMEMBER: ALL THIS IS PERSONAL

A little later, we'll look at in-depth profiles of each archetype. As you read through them, you'll likely notice yourself identifying with one or more, and that's great. You can think of them as equally strong components of your personality, or you can think of them as pieces of a different kind of astrological chart—maybe you're a Queen with Steamroller rising. There's no "right way" to relate to these archetypes. After all, the Mirror Matrix is all about you. At the end of the section we'll talk about each archetype more deeply, but for now keep these five profiles in mind as you read:

- Core

- Secondary

- Aspirational

- Situational

- Toxic

It's natural to start putting the women you know into different archetypes too, and I've listed several women in each, both real and fictional, to help illustrate the traits of the archetype. These examples are not hard and fast; you might disagree, and that's okay. As I was developing the Mirror Matrix, I reached out to my network to get feedback, and it was fascinating to see the fervor of the opinions that came in. Some were annoyed that I had put certain women in one category or another. (Some were annoyed that I had included them on a list of "bitches" at all—even though they knew I was using the term positively in an effort to ditch the stigma and reclaim the word, which just goes to show how powerful that stigma really is.)

This speaks to how subjective our perception of women's behavior is, that our own filters, experiences, values, and priorities tell us which behavior is acceptable, which is not, and who it's acceptable from. That is obviously going to impact how you perceive these profiles that I've put together.

When it comes to our own individual archetypes, there will be similar subjectivity and variation. Any given archetype may look a little different from person to person, but the underlying motivations will be the same. For example, Fanatics might be loud and fiery or cold and calculating, but either way, their goal is to intimidate you into going their way and endorsing their beliefs. These archetypes are not definitive, and you may not agree with all of them, but I want you to see them as a foundation to build from.

CHAPTER 6

Toxic Bitch Behavior

AS WE SAW ABOVE, IT'S important to separate the difference between behavior that is ACTUALLY negative from behaviors that are simply labeled as undesirable based on our society's traditions.

Toxic Bitch behavior includes some of the following characteristics:

- Being catty, snarky, or rude
- Undermining and tearing down other women
- Being unwilling to compromise, no matter the situation
- Nonconsensually controlling a situation
- Being condescending

We're not looking to be rude and just say, "I'm a bitch, I don't care what you think, and you're going to deal with it," because that's not going to get you very far. Besides, that kind of behavior just makes you a jerk, not a badass.

Toxic Femininity

Let's get deeper into the idea of toxic femininity. The most brilliant takedown of toxic femininity I've ever seen is a tweet thread by Kat Blaque from June 2018. In it she lists traits and behaviors that are often listed as toxic femininity and refutes each one.

"Tears are weaponized because women are seen as lesser than men. Obsessing with beauty is often rewarded in a society that sees beauty as a value—one often suggested to be for men. Competing for male attention speaks for itself. It's all femininity reinforced by men. These things all share one thing in common: men. These things are all about men, and not about women defining their femininity for themselves. Which isn't the same as what we refer to as toxic masculinity. Women are rarely the reason men violently seek to reinforce themselves."[31]

Blaque goes on to discuss the idea that "conventions of femininity" are more about internalized misogyny and wouldn't exist without the patriarchy enforcing them.

Ironically, femininity—both toxic and not—is still rooted in misogyny when it is defined in opposition to masculinity rather than existing as a standalone influence. (Femininity on its own can be quite powerful.) In other words, the traits that are bad for men are expected for women. "Appropriate behavior" for women really has nothing to do with what we—women—want or need. To take it even further, toxic femininity is rooted in some women's instincts to blame other women for the sexism they experience.

Let's look at some of the ways women are taught to be toxic, most especially to each other.

Queen of the Mountain Syndrome

Queen of the Mountain Syndrome, which I mentioned in Chapter 3, is what I call the way some women fight for their seats at the table and then actively keep other women from achieving the same.

This is a unique challenge for women, though it's certainly something that other marginalized folks have to deal with as well.

When you're the only Black person in the room and there has traditionally been only one spot for a person of color, you *could* help other people but you might displace yourself. Or if you're a woman and there's one spot in the boardroom for a woman, why would you help promote other women? That might unseat you from your hard-won power.

This is a powerful framework for looking at toxic femininity and the ways that women lash out at one another in order to raise ourselves up.

One common way Queen of the Mountain syndrome presents itself is through "frenemies." This portmanteau of "friend" and "enemy" describes someone who seems like your friend but who is actually out to undermine you in the way an enemy would. As women, we start to develop these relationships at a shockingly young age. When I was a kid, all of my worst bullies were also my best friends, and, looking back, it's shocking to think about how some of these kids were constantly betraying and hurting each other and being catty and condescending in very real ways—even just on the playground.

Ostracism is another technique women use against each other all the time. For a variety of no-good reasons, we deem one woman "not good enough" to be part of the club, and we shut her out, leaving her to fend for herself as we continue working our way to the top.

Another aspect of toxic femininity is the way women actively put other women down in order to set ourselves apart, saying things like, "I'm not like other girls," to show that we don't do the things that women are trashed for doing. Or what about the backhanded compliment? "Oh, I could never wear something like that. But you know, it really suits you."

Women are socialized to let their conflicts fester, to talk about them with others scheming behind each other's backs, and to ice out other women after a disagreement. As messed up as it is, this is how we're taught to deal with things. The way it then translates into our adult lives is Queen of the Mountain Syndrome, where all too many women feel like the only way to hold their places at the top is to push other women back down.

WHAT DOES TOXIC BITCH BEHAVIOR LOOK LIKE?

I ask this question in my workshops, too. Here are just a few of the fantastic answers women have given:

- Being a mean girl
- Not listening
- Tearing down other people
- Being condescending, catty, or backstabbing
- Being physically or verbally aggressive
- Having a bad attitude
- Being overly defensive
- Arrogance
- Being a "Queen Bee"
- Bullying others
- Belittling

- Being dismissive
- Being judgmental
- Dressing down other women
- Self-righteousness
- Cussing someone out versus just cussing
- Screaming and yelling

These behaviors aren't healthy or productive. When I encourage you to act like a bitch, I'm not saying to go in and be arrogant or be backstabbing or to run roughshod over people. That's not going to suddenly turn all of us into more successful women who are allowed to take up space. That's Toxic Bitch behavior.

Toxic Bitch Archetypes

The three "Toxic Bitch" archetypes have many shared traits, but each has its own distinct twists, too.

Sometimes Toxic Bitch behavior is subtle, and sometimes it's overt. Toxic Bitches are often veiled in charm and seriously skilled at gaslighting, acting as if others are just being too sensitive for calling out their bad behavior, or as if there's just been a misunderstanding.

NOT ALL TOXIC BITCH BEHAVIOR IS MALICIOUS, BUT IT IS ALL DAMAGING.

Toxic Bitches are women you do *not* want to model yourself after, who exhibit harmful behavior and might even veer into abusive territory.

Humans are complex, and no one's behavior is black and white. Simply exhibiting toxic behavior doesn't make someone a "bad" person. Though we are never obligated to put up with that toxic behavior, we have to look at patterns, intentions, and context before we judge whether a *person* is toxic. Humans are often operating from a place of unconsciousness and sometimes even deep trauma. It can be easy to think we know why someone is behaving a certain way or to judge based on our own experiences, but, really, it's very rare to fully understand where someone is coming from. Frankly, we're all toxic at some point, and when we can look in the Mirror Matrix and recognize those tendencies in ourselves, it makes it much easier not only to correct our own behavior but to give others the benefit of the doubt. After all, if you know that certain situations trigger your inner Tyrant or that being hangry turns you into an uncontrollable Steamroller, it's easier to remember that women who are *acting* like Toxic Bitches may have things going on behind the scenes that you don't know about.

Let's take a look through the three Toxic Bitch archetypes and see if you can relate them to anyone you know (or maybe yourself, on a bad day).

----------- FANATIC -----------

The Fanatic has strong opinions and wants everyone to know it. Her insistence on being correct is an obstacle to having a mutually respectful conversation, and she can be incredibly dogmatic. She speaks with intensity and relentlessness and could easily be described as an "opinion tornado."

The Fanatic is overly defensive and belittles other people's experiences and opinions if they don't line up with her own. She might have "control freak" tendencies and have a hard time sharing power. The Fanatic is a woman of extremes: she'll either ice you out and give you the cold shoulder or she'll explode in a fiery rage. She can be confrontational, and she might be a screamer when she gets angry.

-------------- MOTTO --------------

"I'm right, and that's just a fact."

-------------- TRAITS --------------

- Opinion tornado
- Relentless
- Unmovable
- Single-focus/Fixated
- Demanding

- Militant
- Rigid/Inflexible
- Aggressive/Volatile
- Underhanded/Manipulative
- Rooted in a belief system
- Opinionated/loud

------ **POP CULTURE EXAMPLES** ------

Cersei Lannister / Game of Thrones

Claire Underwood / House of Cards

Sherry Palmer / 24

Jeanine Pirro - Entertainer

Valerie Solanas - Radical Feminist

Rosanne Barr - Actress

----------- **CHALLENGES** -----------

Off-put doesn't even begin to describe how others feel when the Fanatic gets going about her most passionate beliefs. It seems nearly impossible for others to discuss or debate ideas because of her refusal to even acknowledge other people's perspectives or opinions.

-------- STEAMROLLER --------

The Steamroller is overbearing and impatient and has a major superiority complex, though she might not admit it. She has no need to hear your opinion because hers is obviously so much better. She can often be a micromanager who doesn't trust others to accomplish what she is able to do herself. Her tone is frequently bossy, and if she's in a managerial position she likes to remind her team who's in charge.

She's highly competitive and can undermine those around her. She might see herself as someone who has high standards, but the way she upholds those standards comes across as rigidity and unwillingness to compromise. She believes in brutal honesty, with an emphasis on the "brutal." She's not always malicious, but her behavior is toxic anyway.

---------------- MOTTO ----------------

"As I was saying..."

---------------- TRAITS ----------------

- Doesn't listen
- Condescending
- Overbearing
- Superiority complex/Narcissism

- Competitive
- Micro-manager
- Oblivious
- Dismissive
- Pompous
- Testy/Snappy
- Insensitive

------ **POP CULTURE EXAMPLES** ------

Tracy Flick / Election

Mindy Lahiri / The Mindy Project

Miss Piggy / The Muppets

Sarah Huckabee Sanders – Political Adviser

Jenna Maroney / 30 Rock

----------- **CHALLENGES** -----------

The Steamroller isn't always malicious, but her intent doesn't really matter when she's inadvertently silencing others. If she doesn't let the people around her get a word in edgewise, she won't be respected.

----------- TYRANT -----------

The Tyrant is your typical mean girl, Queen Bee. She's rude, catty, and loves to tear other women down. She can be a bully and is super judgmental. She uses sarcasm for plausible deniability when she's being a jerk. She wields ostracism as a weapon in order to exclude and punish those she's displeased with. She tends toward clique-ish behavior and can be hostile. She generally avoids communication, unless she sees an opportunity to be snarky.

The Tyrant isn't interested in helping others make progress and is liable to sabotage anyone in her way. This archetype is most associated with Toxic Bitch behavior.

------------- MOTTO -------------

"I'm going to crush you."

------------- TRAITS -------------

- Rude/Catty
- Arrogant
- Manipulative
- Hardened
- Domineering
- Temperamental

- Secretive
- Demeaning/Uses humiliation

------ **POP CULTURE EXAMPLES** ------

Heather Chandler / Heathers

Regina George / Mean Girls

Miranda / The Devil Wears Prada

Santana Lopez / Glee

Endora / Bewitched

Elektra / Pose

Scarlett O'Hara / Gone With the Wind

Joan Crawford - Actress

----------- **CHALLENGES** -----------

Everyone around the Tyrant feels awful, demeaned, and degraded. She's super toxic and, frankly, nobody likes her, but they do fear her. That may be a strength or a weakness depending on your viewpoint. (I see it as weakness.)

GO DEEPER: WHAT'S YOUR EXPERIENCE WITH TOXIC BITCH BEHAVIOR?

- List a few examples of badly behaving women. Who *don't* you want to be like? Why?

- What toxic behaviors have you seen directed towards you or others?

- What toxic behaviors have you participated in?

- Are there certain environments where you see more Toxic Bitch behavior than in others?

- Why do you think women often treat other women so poorly?

- What can we do to deemphasize these behaviors within our own groups of friends or colleagues?

- Visit BitchStigma.com/Library for downloadable grids, profiles and more resources.

CHAPTER 7

Bold Badass Behavior

AS YOU KNOW, IT'S NOT just toxic behavior that gets labeled as bitchy. Women are also labeled a bitch for behaviors that are GOOD and STRONG! I call these women Bold Badasses.

Bold Badass behavior includes just a few of these confident choices:

- Setting and maintaining boundaries (saying no!)
- Speaking directly and not sugar-coating your words
- Not allowing others to speak over you
- Being ambitious
- Responding firmly to someone ELSE's rude behavior

While all these things may get us labeled a bitch, they are actually very healthy behaviors.

"Better bitch than mouse."

—RUTH BADER GINSBURG, ASSOCIATE JUSTICE OF THE
SUPREME COURT OF THE UNITED STATES

When I asked the women in my workshops about the healthy, strong, positive things women do that *still* might get them labeled a bitch, this is what they said:

- Communicating clearly and directly
- Being confident and believing in ourselves
- Saying no
- Setting boundaries in general but especially rejecting anyone who ignores those boundaries. Whether it's a colleague's idea or a romantic overture, saying no tends to get us moved into the bitch category very quickly
- Being abrupt or curt and not wrapping everything we're saying in bubble wrap to soften its landing in someone's sweet little ears
- Asking for what we're worth, knowing our value, and expressing it concretely
- Letting other people be uncomfortable instead of immediately soothing those around us
- Speaking up when something is offensive—that gets us labeled sensitive *and* bitchy
- Standing in our truth
- Being ambitious
- Wanting *more* in life or our professions
- Wanting to "have it all"
- Being passionate—simply having a fire in our bellies about something
- Being persistent
- Being the only person to speak up
- Being knowledgeable

- Taking the time you need for yourself
- Standing up for someone who might not be very popular

Bold Badass Archetypes

The whole point is that the women expressing these behaviors *aren't* bitches, at least not in the toxic sense. Their attitudes and behaviors are often misconstrued, misunderstood, and misrepresented, but their strengths and skills are actually healthy.

All of the Bold Badass archetypes share some traits: they are unapologetic, independent, ambitious, strong-willed, and strong-voiced. The differences lie in the nuances of the energy and presentation. Think of it as various flavors of confidence, and choose the ones that best suit you.

Let me say it one more time for the people in the back: these women, especially the real life examples, are *not* bitches in the toxic, derogatory sense of the word. These nonconformist women exhibit strength, grace, clarity, and more, and I find them to be incredibly inspirational. That's what the Bold Badass archetypes are all about: finding inspiration, reflecting on our power, and exploring the diverse ways to be confident in this world.

You can embody different archetypes at different times depending on the situation, how you're feeling, and what's warranted (remember the Five Profiles from the last chapter?). There are also a lot of overlapping traits that might be applicable for multiple archetypes.

Your goal should be to become the best, strongest version of who you are. One or more of these archetypes might resonate with you now, or they may be more aspirational, highlighting a kind of energy you want to learn to embody.

---------- ADVOCATE ----------

The Advocate is polite and principled and gains her strength from knowing she's doing the right thing. She rises up and makes her voice heard in service of fighting for herself or, even more likely, others. The Advocate is very matter-of-fact with strong argumentative skills, and she tends to have an academic or professional background. Generally, she's very even-keeled, but she can get heated when she feels that something important is being overlooked.

The Advocate can be a great leader and tends to take a collaborative approach. She isn't a leader for power's sake; she genuinely wants to help. She can become ferocious when the situation (or her knowledge and expertise) is being inappropriately dismissed, which then requires her to assert herself. It's very important to her to "do the right thing," and she feels very integrity driven.

-------------- MOTTO --------------

"I fight for others, so you won't silence me."

-------------- TRAITS --------------

- Polite, tactful, formal
- Principled
- Chooses her battles

- Honest, straightforward
- Academic
- Integrity-driven
- Otherwise mild-mannered
- Does the "right thing" even when it's the hard thing

-------- **POP CULTURE EXAMPLES** --------

Alice Walker - Poet and Activist

Jane Fonda - Actress and Activist

Supergirl

Leslie Knope/ Parks & Rec

Janet Mock – Writer and Activist

Rachel Maddow – Television host

Gloria Steinem – Journalist and Author

Clair Huxtable / The Cosby Show

Julia Sugarbaker / Designing Women

Laverne Cox - Actress and Advocate

------------ **CHALLENGES** ------------

She's often underestimated, and because she's polite she can be misunderstood as a bit of a Pollyanna. Then when her ferociousness comes out, the people around her are confused and taken aback. This is a classic case of how anytime a woman steps "out of line" the perception of her might move into bitch territory. Usually she's really pleasant, so when she sets a boundary in any way, people start to think she's being bitchy.

---------- **TOXIC POTENTIAL** ----------

Fanatic, Steamroller

WARRIOR

The Warrior is a fierce fighter and will use whatever tools are necessary and available to speak up and speak out. She defends herself and others and can be ruthless if the situation calls for it. She is vigilant, tireless, and unwilling to tolerate any bullshit from the world around her. She often has one or more specific convictions that she will uphold intensely.

The Warrior can wield anger like a sharp knife and can be impatient with those who would rather take a more diplomatic approach. She doesn't have time to play at politics; her focus is on resisting being silenced and being a force for change. She sticks up for what she believes in, no matter the cost or the consequences.

MOTTO

"I will unapologetically do whatever I need to do."

TRAITS

- Fierce
- Tireless/relentless
- Vigilant
- Passionate

- Intensely convicted
- Persistent/Perseverent
- Committed to a cause
- Action-driven
- Brave/Proud
- Fiercely loyal

POP CULTURE EXAMPLES

Jessica Jones /Marvel

Blanca / Pose

Gemma / Sons of Anarchy

Arya Stark / Game of Thrones

Megan Rapinoe - Soccer Player

Annalise Keating / How to Get Away with Murder

CHALLENGES

Her intensity can easily lead her into Tyrant mode. She's willing to do anything (seriously, almost anything) to fight for what she believes is right. She can get impatient working within the system and lash out at her own allies.

TOXIC POTENTIAL

Fanatic, Tyrant

----------- QUEEN ------------

The Queen is aloof, remote, and self-contained, three traits that are often misunderstood as being snobby or unfriendly. She is a woman of few words and doesn't feel the need to comfort others with inconsequential chatter. A definite introvert, she can tend to be a bit of a loner. When she does talk, she's thoughtful and direct and expresses her deep, meaningful beliefs. The Queen is a quiet powerhouse who can assert her beliefs without raising her voice or getting all worked up.

----------- MOTTO -----------

"I don't need to entertain you.
I'll speak when I'm ready."

-------------- TRAITS -------------

- Enigmatic
- Dignified
- Aloof/Remote
- Self-contained
- Woman of few words
- Diplomatic
- Observant/Contemplative
- Imposing

- - - - - - - POP CULTURE EXAMPLES - - - - - - -

Wanda von Dunajew / Venus in Furs

Melinda May / Agents of SHIELD

Letty Ortiz / Fast and the Furious

Sansa Stark / Game of Thrones

Furiosa / Mad Max: Fury Road

Angelina Jolie - Actress and Activist

Lady Gaga - Singer and Actress

Anna Wintour - Vogue Editor

Rihanna - Singer, Actress, Entrepreneur

- - - - - - - - - - - CHALLENGES - - - - - - - - - - -

She can appear *too* mysterious and seem completely unknowable. Others are intimidated by her quietness. She can be seen as an "ice queen," and that can make her both feel and appear isolated.

- - - - - - - - - - TOXIC POTENTIAL - - - - - - - - - -

Tyrant

----------- BOSS -----------

The Boss's confidence is rooted in her competency, which others often find threatening. She's sharp and no-nonsense and uses hierarchy to support her natural leadership skills. She might be described as cold or heartless, but really she's focused on efficiency and achievement and doesn't waste time with small talk or small ideas.
The Boss believes in establishing protocols and executing best practices and processes. She expects those around her to fulfill their commitments and isn't interested in excuses or mollycoddling anyone, whether professionally or personally.

----------- MOTTO -----------

"Because I said so..."

----------- TRAITS -----------

- Competent/Skillful
- In charge
- Hierarchal
- Collaborative
- Brusque/No-nonsense
- Enforces protocols
- Accomplished

- Action-driven
- Authoritative
- Assumes leadership easily

------- **POP CULTURE EXAMPLES** -------

Kamala Harris - Politician

Martha Stewart - TV Host

Olivia / Scandal

Captain Janeway / Star Trek

Christina Yang / Grey's Anatomy

Jessica Pearson / Suits

Hillary Clinton - Former Secretary of State

Jackie / Nurse Jackie

----------- **CHALLENGES** -----------

She can forget that the "small talk" that she hates is important to relationship building. Her impatience with social niceties can backfire. She's confident with leadership and is ambitious, which can be seen as negative traits in a woman specifically.

---------- **TOXIC POTENTIAL** ----------

Steamroller, Tyrant

------------ REBEL ------------

The Rebel embraces her originality and can be a trailblazer, intentionally or not. She uses unapologetic charm and wit to get her point across and never backs down from a challenge. She's often seen as "cool" and quite obviously marches to the beat of her own drum. The Rebel is blunt and independent and doesn't respect authority for authority's sake. She understands that others may misunderstand her intent, but that doesn't slow her down or stop her from pursuing her passions.

------------ MOTTO ------------

"I'm doing my own thing. You can come with or get out of the way."

------------ TRAITS ------------

- Blunt
- Self-possessed
- Trailblazing/Pioneering
- Charming/Influential
- Rebellious
- Edgy
- Outspoken

------- POP CULTURE EXAMPLES -------

Angela Davis - Author and Activist

P!nk - Singer

Emma Gonzalez - Activist

Frida Kahlo - Artist

Margaret Cho - Comedian

Blanche Devereaux / Golden Girls

Roxane Gay - Author

Lizzo - Singer

Chrissy Teigen - Model

Natalie Wynn / ContraPoints

Veronica Mars / Veronica Mars

Pippi Longstocking

----------- CHALLENGES -----------

She's outside of the box but still in the system. The Rebel can struggle with still wanting to be seen as likable, so she can feel conflicted about speaking out more firmly.

--------- TOXIC POTENTIAL ---------

Steamroller, Tyrant

ROGUE

The Rogue is the edgiest and most intense profile. She's revolutionary, radical, and incredibly sharp-tongued. She doesn't care at all for social niceties and feels it's a waste of time to cater to the unenlightened. She probably enjoys vulgarity (in public or private or both). She really doesn't care if others find her likable, because she ferociously believes in what she's saying or doing.

The Rogue wears the "bitch" label with pride. Her philosophy is, "If you can't stand the heat, get out of the kitchen," and she refuses to minimize herself for the comfort of others. She is a truth-teller even when it's hard, and she will not just speak truth to power, but shout it.

MOTTO

"I don't care if you like me, but you'll hear what I have to say."

TRAITS

- Unorthodox
- Radical/Non-conformist
- Sharp-tongued/Snarky
- Truth-teller
- Anti-establishment

- Anti-authority
- Takes no prisoners
- Unapologetic
- Hard-nosed

POP CULTURE EXAMPLES

Madonna - Singer

Nicki Minaj - Singer

Lil' Kim - Singer

Pam DeBeaufort / True Blood

Cookie / Empire

Margo / The Magicians

Faith / Buffy the Vampire Slayer

Sandra Bernhard - Comedian

Maxine Waters - Politician

Alexandria Ocasio-Cortez - Politician

CHALLENGES

The Rogue can have a hard time working with others and is more of a one-woman show than a collaborator. Her sharp edges can be off-putting, and her impatience can reach toxic levels. She can seem hard as nails but might secretly be sensitive. She naturally challenges authority and that can undermine her progress. When she is really fired up she can be like a bull in a china shop.

---------**TOXIC POTENTIAL**----------

Fanatic, Steamroller, Tyrant

Your Five Archetypes

Ok, so now that you've read through all the archetypes, which ones do you feel most connected to? Which ones do you see in the mirror every morning? Which ones do you catch glimpses of in certain situations? Which ones would you like to see more of?

Core - This is your most natural archetype. The one that most deeply resonates. When you read it you think, "Yep, that's me." Your core profile is who you are at your baseline, when you're happy and confident.

Secondary - Your secondary archetype is the one you can also see yourself in, but not as frequently. It also comes pretty naturally to you (or you've learned to work at it and make it happen).

Aspirational - We all have traits that we would like to improve, or at least have access to, and your aspirational archetype includes those elements. In a later chapter we'll discuss how to strengthen those traits within yourself.

Situational - This is the archetype (or multiple archetypes) that you can draw on depending on the situation. At work, in public space, with friends or family—each can present different requirements for the way you communicate and handle yourself.

Toxic - There's no shame in the fact that we're not always at our best. We're only human, and sometimes that means we slide into toxic territory, especially when we're feeling the need to defend ourselves. This is the archetype that you're most likely to embody as a coping mechanism if you're upset, stressed, or triggered.

TAKE ACTION: WHICH BITCH ARE YOU?

- Make a list of how you see yourself, and remember that you are the one who defines yourself. It's your own reflection you're worried about here—not what anyone else sees when they look at you.

- But as we've mentioned, self-reflection is important for every kind of bitch. Make a list of how you think others see you.

- On both lists, put a check mark next to the traits you think are accurate and an X next to the ones that aren't.

- Now, highlight the traits (accurate or not) that you want to embody, and add any others you'd like to develop.

Visit www.BitchStigma.com/Library for downloadable grids, profiles, and more resources.

ADVOCATE	WARRIOR	FANATIC
QUEEN	BOSS	STEAMROLLER
REBEL	ROGUE	TYRANT

SECTION 3
THE BITCH MINDSET

*"Nothing I accept about myself can be
used against me to diminish me."*

—AUDRE LORDE, WRITER

NOW THAT YOU HAVE HAD a thorough introduction to the Mirror
Matrix, it's time to start creating the mindset that will boost the
badass you already are, or help you integrate a new attitude into
your life.

CHAPTER 8

Who Gets to Decide If You're Being a Toxic Bitch or a Bold Badass?

"Take criticism seriously, but not personally. If there is truth or merit in the criticism, try to learn from it. Otherwise, let it roll right off you."

—HILLARY CLINTON, FORMER SECRETARY OF STATE

WE TALKED EARLIER IN THE book about how important it is to work from the inside out and to stop prioritizing what OTHER people think of your behavior, but that's easier said than done.

A common question I hear is: "What do I do when someone thinks I'm a bitch or calls me a bitch? Like, what do I actually do? I'm aware of the situation, but how do I respond to it?"

Let's say that you're dealing with a situation where someone is accusing you of being one of the Toxic Bitch archetypes (or being difficult, or any number of other more business-appropriate insults), but you feel certain that you're actually being bold and setting healthy boundaries. This chapter is going to help you develop an assessment tool to identify how to respond in a situation when someone accuses you of being a bitch.

THE FIRST STEP IS ASSESSING WHO THE PERSON IS AND HOW MUCH IMPACT THEY'RE GOING TO HAVE ON YOUR CAREER OR LIFE.

There are various levels of impact. Having colleagues think that you're a bitch could be a mere annoyance, or it could impact the teams you're assigned to and the promotion opportunities you get. It depends on what your individual work environment is.

Is there wiggle room for someone to simply think you're a bitch without having any impact on your career? In that case, how can you start to let go of your concerns about how they feel? How can you start interacting with them as pleasantly as possible without overextending yourself in your efforts to control their perception?

That's one level. But if the person could truly have an impact on your career path, that's another story. Maybe the person in question is a colleague who influences a team project, or maybe they have more seniority, or they're somebody who is moving up the hierarchy and has let that little bit of power go to their head.

In any case, if it's someone who can have a significant effect on your career—or any other aspect of your life—then you'll likely need to figure out what's happening and work to cultivate a more positive interaction *without* compromising your needs.

This is where direct communication from a place of compassion comes in.

It's easy to come into the conversation with a big attitude, but instead try hard to approach it with curious compassion and a little bit of distance. You're looking for information, but you're not looking for validation, and I think that's an important differentiator. Go up and say, "Hey, I'm really curious about what's going on. I want to check and see if there's anything that we can talk about to improve this situation, or this relationship, or this bump in the road."

It's important to remember that you can (and should) do that without coming in and self-flagellating. Don't go in with an attitude of, "Oh, I must have done something so awful for you to think this or to say this." Don't come in with the apologies right off the bat either. You can certainly express regret that the situation is less than amicable, but there is no need to apologize for looking out for yourself. In short, approach the situation with curiosity and not apology.

How Do Power Dynamics Factor In?

In order to approach this conversation most effectively—so that the other person will be willing to truly listen—you'll want to take some time to analyze the power dynamics at play.

Power dynamics are a core aspect of kink that have helped me see all the ways that people jockey for power in their everyday lives. In kink exploration, the act of consensually and conscientiously giving up or taking over control is a way of putting boundaries around the natural human tendency to figure out who "leads the pack." Contrary to popular belief, it's possible to be the most powerful person in the room, and yet not be the most obviously dominant.

Power dynamics affect nearly every single interpersonal experience we have. Sometimes these dynamics are subtle and don't impact the relationship, but other times the need to be in the power position completely dictates someone's behavior—even if they're not aware of it. With those people it's important to understand power dynamics and to try to see what's motivating their perception of power. That's how you know which angle to approach them from.

Some people really are very invested in the power of a title, but they're not necessarily interested in doing the work required of that position. In that case, their interest in the perception of power becomes a point of entry for the conversation. If they're more interested in hierarchy, then making sure they know you're not trying to outrank them would be important. That's going to color your approach.

"Though maintaining an atmosphere of community rather than hierarchy may have advantages in some settings, people who are not afraid of conflict have an advantage in innumerable inevitable situations where others try to get their way. Being willing to make a scene can be an effective form of power."

— DEBORAH TANNEN[32]

Power dynamics are a big part of whether people think you're a bitch or not. Men are often socialized to have a very hierarchical thinking, so if they think you're trying to outrank them, they feel threatened. If you're trying to act like you're better than them, (or you are actually better than them), or your title is better than theirs, then that's going to influence the way they think of you and your approach, no matter how you're actually behaving.

That attitude is very different from people who are socialized in a feminine way and tend to have a more backchannel approach to things. Women tend to be socialized around community building, so they might think you're a bitch if they perceive that you're not a team player. If you wanted to start a conversation to try to deal with the friction, you'd approach this person very differently than the one who feels his hierarchical position is threatened.

When you feel the Bitch Stigma getting in the way of your confidence, the first thing to do is to ask yourself this question: who is accusing you (in reality or in your mind) of being a bitch and do they matter in your life?

Are you just simply doing what you need to do and they're unhappy about it? In that case, you need to allow them to have their own experience and not feel responsible for changing the situation. The assessment tool below will help you determine whether this person's perspective should impact your behavior.

Priority Assessment Tool

The fact is, certain people's opinions *should* have more weight than other people's in your life. That's not a rude thing; that's a survival thing.

Here are some questions to consider when evaluating someone's opinion of you, whether it's a colleague, family member, or friend.

- Does this person have power over my life?
  - ○ A: Not at all
  - ○ B: Only in certain settings
  - ○ C: Yes, significant power

- Is this relationship important to me?
  - ○ A: Not at all
  - ○ B: In some ways
  - ○ C: Yes, very
- Is this relationship necessary?
  - ○ A: Nope
  - ○ B: Sometimes I think so
  - ○ C: Yes, definitely
- Do I care about this person's opinion of me?
  - ○ A: Not a bit
  - ○ B: In certain situations
  - ○ C: Yes, very much
- Is this a short-term or long-term relationship?
  - ○ A: Very short-term
  - ○ B: We'll have to interact regularly for a while
  - ○ C: Long-term
- Are they educated on the subject?
  - ○ A: They have no idea what they're talking about
  - ○ B: They know about as much as I do
  - ○ C: They're experts
- Are they offering any constructive feedback?
  - ○ A: None
  - ○ B: About some things
  - ○ C: Yes, their feedback is always constructive
- Are they genuinely trying to help me/lift me/support me/build me up?

○ A: No

○ B: Sometimes

○ C: Always

TAKE ACTION: SHOULD YOU CONSIDER THEIR OPINION?

Pick someone who you've had a conflict with. Answer each of the above questions, and then tally your answers.

A._____

B._____

C._____

If you answered mostly A's and B's, they aren't worth your concern. If you answered mostly B's and C's, it may be worth trying to find a solution.

Did they end up being worth your concern? Then let's consider the consequences of what would happen if this person thinks you're being a Toxic Bitch. At the top of a piece of paper, write or type: What would happen if_____thought I was being a Toxic Bitch?

If you've determined that the person in question has an opinion worth caring about and that the consequences of him (or her) thinking you're a bitch are significant enough to want to avoid, then it's time to have a conversation about how to create a mutually respectful relationship. Consider the power dynamics driving this person's perspective and use that information to plan the most effective approach. **Remember, be curious, compassionate, and confident.**

CHAPTER 9

Sitting with Discomfort—Good Pain Is Transformative

"Courage is not the absence of fear, but rather the judgement that something else is more important than fear."

—AMBROSE REDMOON, WRITER

A BIG PART OF DITCHING the Bitch Stigma and the fear of that stigma is learning to sit with the right kind of discomfort.

Difficult conversations are, well, difficult, and most people avoid them with every ounce of their being. We have to be prepared for rejection just for trying to broach a tough subject.

Preparing for rejection and sitting with discomfort are two things that are going to end up being a big part of this journey, because you *will* be uncomfortable. It is uncomfortable to try to talk about emotions that are not utterly positive. Most of us are not given the tools to do that in our lives. We're not taught in school how to navigate difficult conversations or complicated relationships.

At its core, most kinky activities are about transforming "bad pain" into "good pain" and that can be one of the most confusing aspects for non-kinky people. Why in the world would someone want to experience the pain of a consensual spanking or flogging? Why would someone want to be all bound up into contortionist positions with rope? **But in kink, the discomfort is often the point. Leaning into discomfort or outright pain can be cathartic and empowering.**

Let's say somebody has called you a bitch (or some version of that, or is treating you that way even if they haven't verbalized it). I'm a big fan of just saying, "Hey, can we talk about what's going on?" I try to keep a pleasant, lighthearted tone about it, though that's not always easy. It can be hard to moderate our tone of voice, especially if we're feeling defensive.

Based on my experience, both in my own body as a woman in the world, and with the hundreds and hundreds of women I have spoken with, anxiety is a real issue that is rooted in the fear of how our behavior is going to be perceived. A lot of women spend a lot of time being uncomfortable already, trying to figure out what other people are thinking, how they're going to perceive our behavior, and what the potential consequences are going to be.

You're likely already sitting with the discomfort of trying to manage everyone else's expectations (which is an impossible task). It's time to shift that discomfort to a more productive kind. **Allow yourself to be uncomfortable with NOT trying to manage other people's perceptions.**

This anxiety is a natural response to changing a lifetime of socialization that requires you to manage and cater to everyone else's emotional state and emotional well-being. Part of the process of learning to sit with this anxiety is overcoming your own internal judgment for prioritizing yourself. Another is brushing off accusations of selfishness, which are just another way to keep women focused on caring for others. "Selfish" is often said with a bit of a roguish tone when it's used to describe men, but when we as women are selfish there's a lot of disdain attached.

There is pain in growth. It's important to look at where we can push that growth in ourselves and in the people around us, but we also need to understand that we are working within a system that is slow to make progress. The only way those social structures and social expectations change is when people refuse to live by the old rules.

"The first problem for all of us, men and women, is not to learn, but to unlearn."

—GLORIA STEINEM, JOURNALIST

Think of it like going to the gym or changing your diet. It's not that those things are easy (otherwise everyone would do it!) but they require a change of perspective and a willingness to experience temporary discomfort in the pursuit of a better future.

How Do We Learn to Embrace Discomfort?

Let's break the process down.

Step one: You have to change your relationship to discomfort. Instead of seeing it as something to avoid, embrace it as a sign of positive change. You have to grow and take steps to reach your goal, but they don't need to be huge steps to get you started. Make your steps manageable so that you can feel successful. Success begets success. When you achieve something once, it becomes easier and easier to achieve it again.

"The steps you take don't need to be big—they just need to take you in the right direction."

—JEMMA, *AGENTS OF SHIELD*[33]

One great step to start with is changing the language you use about yourself. Words matter, and they're a powerful influence on how we think and what we believe. Try to cut out negative words like "can't," "difficult," and "impossible." Replace them with positive words like "try," "can," and "achieve."

Recognize your fear and discomfort and make space for it. The more you try to push it down, the greater its hold on you will be. It's completely normal to feel fear or anxiety when you're making a change in your life, but you have the choice to take action anyway.

"Stay afraid, but do it anyway. What's important is the action. You don't have to wait to be confident. Just do it, and eventually the confidence will follow."

—CARRIE FISHER, ACTRESS

Step two: Take action! Don't let "blender brain" (aka when your brain goes round and round on a single subject without getting anywhere) get you stuck in your own thought process. When you take action and start making changes, your own progress will inspire you to keep going.

Step three: Do it all over again. **This is all about building resilience.** You have to believe that you will make it through the discomfort to a better life on the other side. As Thomas Jefferson allegedly said, "If you want something in life that you have never had, you will have to do something that you have never done."

In order to get comfortable feeling uncomfortable, you have to seek out things that push your limits. Repetitious expansion of your comfort zone creates opportunity for deep growth. To be truly successful, don't just tolerate discomfort, embrace it.

Dealing with Anxiety About & Toxic Responses to Changing Behavior

I want to be very clear that I personally continue to struggle with the Bitch Stigma. I love talking to women who have either never felt the Bitch Stigma or who have completely gotten over it, but those women have been few and far between. Even having been so entrenched in discussing the impact of stigma, I have days when I'm feeling my confident, centered, Badass Rogue identity and many other days when I'm not.

Confidence is a journey, not a destination. It's not a place you are going to land in perfectly. Even Brené Brown, who literally wrote the book on using vulnerability as a strength, shared in her 2019 Netflix special, *The Call to Courage,* that she still experiences the struggle around her vulnerability.[34]

If it's okay for Brené to struggle, it's okay for me and it's okay for you.

I think it's important for strong women to remember that it's not a matter of feeling perfectly accepting of ourselves. If you do achieve that, that's amazing, and I want to find out what you're doing, because it's incredible. But I want to make sure women don't feel like total self-acceptance is the end-all-be-all or that; As the author of this book, I've somehow reached the pinnacle of never feeling iffy about my assertiveness. I think that the world we live in, and the messages we have been internalizing for an exceptionally long time, don't just disappear overnight or even in a decade.

If you're someone who feels the strength of steel sometimes, and feels a deeper struggle other times, know that it's okay. Know that it's natural and normal. Give yourself a bit of a break, whether you're being bitchy or whether you're being softer.

That's part of the process of embracing discomfort and owning your inner badass.

This Shouldn't Be Torture Though

It's one thing to push your boundaries and expand your skills and comfort zone, but it's another to cause yourself panic attacks, or ruin important relationships, or negatively impact your career. It's up to YOU to decide how these techniques fit into your life.

This isn't about doing a complete renovation of your life and your personality. You're much more likely to find success when you take small steps to create a sense of achievement. Don't dive into the deep end and try to overhaul every single way you communicate, because it's easy to feel overwhelmed and give up, and continue with avoidance patterns. (Besides, approaching this journey as a complete overhaul totally discounts all the amazing, healthy, confident things you're *already doing.*)

As you work to make these changes, practicing will be like exposure therapy. By exerting your new skills in no-pressure and low-pressure situations, you can build the confidence you need to try them out in larger situations. If you're forced to confront a huge fear all at once, it's possible it will leave you traumatized and unwilling to try again.

As you practice, remember that it's okay to mess up! You might give these techniques a try and still stick your foot in your mouth or stumble over what you're trying to say. Sometimes you'll do everything right and people *still* won't listen.

This is about perseverance and resilience, and when you build both of those things slowly, they become a super strong foundation to continue building on. This develops into what is called "habituation," meaning that, over time, you'll find your reactions to your fears decrease and become more manageable.

The key is repetition and consistency. Don't try it once and then wait a year to try again. This is about strengthening the confidence muscle: if you don't exercise it, it atrophies. It's a wash, rinse, repeat cycle. That's how the act of speaking up and speaking your truth becomes a natural response—something you'll eventually be able to do without thinking twice about it. (We'll talk later about building a support network and finding exercises that will help you create this consistency.)

I still get nervous when I have to confront someone or when I need to speak up in a spontaneous situation, but I've learned to push past the knot in my stomach and do it anyway.

GO DEEPER: GETTING COMFORTABLE WITH DISCOMFORT

- How do you currently deal with discomfort?

- Think about a time you made a big change in your life (whether you were saving money, building healthy habits, learning a new skill, or anything else). What strategies worked well for you, and how will you use that experience to inform this new initiative?

- What are the first changes you're going to make on your journey to embracing your inner badass?

CHAPTER 10

Your Inner Doomsday Machine

WE ALL HAVE AN INNER monologue, but for some of us that voice sounds more like an Inner Doomsday Machine (IDM) than a cheerleading squad. This voice can be one of the biggest contributors to our inner Bitch Stigma, so let's talk about some ways to deal with it and, if not shut it up, then at least quiet it down.

The Inner Doomsday Machine is that voice in your head that is always focused on the worst possible outcome of any given action. It's made up of your own fears and socializations, along with looping tracks from the naysayers in your life—people who talk down to you or about you.

In *The Call to Courage*, Brené Brown talks about using the phrase, "The story I'm telling myself is..." to remind ourselves that we might be concocting a story that has no basis in reality.[35] Your IDM *might* be responding to what's actually happening, but it's more likely to be rooted in anxiety and catastrophizing.

"Everyone thinks you're being a total bitch right now."

"You know you sound bitchy, and that's why no one respects you."

"If you're demanding then no one will like you, and you'll end up alone."

Our Inner Doomsday Machine and the stories it tells is one of the biggest contributors to the power the Bitch Stigma holds over us.

So we're going to talk about the different aspects of the Inner Doomsday Machine, and then we're going to talk about how to put it away—or, if you're so inclined, how to dismantle it and take it apart piece by piece and crush it with a hammer.

First, let's see if we can identify why that doomsday voice is the way it is. In her book, *The Secret Thoughts of Successful Women,* Dr. Valerie Young identifies five "competence types" that can be helpful in identifying patterns or bad habits that may be holding you back from your full potential:[36]

1. Perfectionism - feels like their work must be completely perfect 100% of the time. It's easy to focus on excessively high goals and then experience major self doubt about measuring up.

2. The Superwoman - tends towards being a workaholic and feels guilty for having downtime. Productivity is the main driver of self worth.

3. The Natural Genius - spent their early years excelling without much effort. In their adult years they avoid challenges because it's uncomfortable trying something that they're "just not good at."

4. The Soloist - doesn't want to ask for help and firmly believes that if they don't do it on their own then it's not worthwhile.

5. The Expert - feels like they never know enough, and fears being exposed as inexperienced or unknowledgeable.

That last one, "The Expert," is a biggie, and it's also known as imposter syndrome. Imposter syndrome, which has become a popular topic in the last few years, refers to this feeling that no matter how accomplished we are, we're still just newbies, and somebody's going to out us as a fraud at any moment. (You won't be surprised to know imposter syndrome affects women far more often than men.)

Each of these patterns contributes to your Inner Doomsday Machine, and when you identify yourself in one of them, you'll likely be able to hear some of your IDM's favorite phrases playing in your head.

Your Inner Doomsday Machine might be telling you how badly others are judging you. It might be telling you that others think you're toxic (even if there's no proof that they think that). Your IDM might be telling you that if you "act like a bitch," no one is going to like you or respect you. But all of those things are based on feelings, not facts. Feelings can be vague and undefined, and sometimes that's what makes them paralyzing.

Let's stop for a moment and figure out exactly what your IDM is saying to you so we can actively counteract it.

Making Your Inner Doomsday Machine Tangible

Since our Inner Doomsday Machines run constantly in the background of our minds, you probably know some of what yours says, but not everything. Or you may have a tough time getting the words on paper or letting your Inner Doomsday Machine speak clearly enough for you to get it out. But making this voice concrete can be extremely helpful in combating it.

In the kink world, we know that denying someone of one or more of their senses can heighten other senses in a powerful way. By blocking out your sensory intake, you can focus on the world inside of you and bring a more productive and acute awareness to your inner responses. Blindfolds are the most recognizable examples of this, but kinksters also use other tools like full head hoods, gags, and immobilizing bondage. It may look weird to outsiders, but kinksters know that it's a trick to true focus.

There are much simpler, non-kinky ways to access the benefits of sensory deprivation that don't require leather and lace.

TAKE ACTION: SENSORY DEPRIVATION AS A TOOL FOR FOCUS

If you don't usually have any visual impairment, blindfolds are a simple tool that often don't have to have anything to do with kink. I use one when I sleep to signal to my brain that it's time to power down and let the day go.

Step one: Either sit at a desk with a notebook and pen or at your computer (it's easier if you type). It might be helpful to have non-lyrical music in the background, or you might prefer silence to keep your focus on your inner voice.

Step two: Put the blindfold on and take some deep breaths. This is going to feel strange at first but let yourself sit with the discomfort (try some affirmations from the next chapter if you need to) and breathe through it.

Step three: Now start writing out your fears and anxieties. There's nothing fancy about this—make it as stream of consciousness as possible. You want to purge and document the untruths that your IDM is running in the background of your mind.

The blindfold is meant to prevent the visual cortex from registering what you're writing and kicking in with the negative judgment and self-editing.

Here are some questions you can ponder during this exercise, just to get you started:

- What am I afraid people will say about me?
- What negative beliefs do I have about "strong women" that are holding me back?
- How does my inner voice speak down to me rather than lifting me up?
- How does my IDM convince me to play small rather than living a large, full life?

Not into wearing a blindfold and/or writing? For those without a usual hearing impairment, you can do this as an audio and verbal combination. Try this exercise instead (or do them both if you really want to dig into these thoughts).

Step One: Go to a private place where you can be alone—somewhere you won't be disturbed and where you will be safe without your hearing and you won't worry about being heard.

Step Two: Put on headphones and pick your favorite music—something that puts you in a state of flow—and turn it up as loud as you can stand without damaging your hearing.

Step three: Use an audio recorder or a voice recording app (or voice to text) on your phone to record yourself talking about the things that bother you. Speak about your fears while you're listening to loud music, so you can't hear yourself talk. Let your words flow without restricting yourself.

GO DEEPER: GETTING TO KNOW YOUR INNER DOOMSDAY MACHINE

- What does your Inner Doomsday Machine say to you?

- What does it look like?

- How did it feel to express your fears without letting your brain and your IDM get in the way?

Dismantling Your Inner Doomsday Machine

Now it's time to take your writings or your voice-to-text files and take a look at them. I'm kind of old-school, so I like to make a bit of an art project of it, but you can keep it simple too.

Go through all of the IDM thoughts, and then write over them with the new confidence boosting thoughts you want to replace them with. Draw circles and cross words out, doodle, and write bold affirmations. You could even create a vision board directly over the writings. Your goal here is to draw such a clear, subconscious line between the negative BS that runs through your brain and your new, positive mantras that, as soon as your IDM starts talking, you can replace its negativity with your own positive thoughts. Have fun with it, and it will become something to refer back to in case your IDM dismantling needs some refreshing.

How do you decide which confident thoughts to write over your IDM's favorite slogans?

AFFIRMATIONS

Affirmations (also sometimes referred to as mantras) are often met with mixed feelings if not outright disdain. But the bottom line is that they work. It's like retraining your brain. (And it's free!)

Quieting our doomsday monologues means changing the way we talk to ourselves. And changing the way we talk to ourselves means changing the messages we focus on. Affirmations are an old-school method that really works. If you've never tried affirmations before, you might feel silly (or maybe you've already tried them and stopped because you felt silly), but if you stick with them, you'll find they can really make an impact on your mindset.

I like to write out a handful (or more) of my favorite affirmations or quotes on index cards so that I can carry one with me for the day or flip through them if I'm feeling super anxious.

There are a few things to remember when coming up with an affirmation:

- Focus on positive words. It's better to say, "I am confident" than "I don't doubt myself."

- If you're going to use a "negative" word, then make sure you include something transformative in the statement. What is the negativity turning into?

- Be sure your affirmations are true. It's okay for your affirmations to be aspirational, but if they're flat-out false, you'll find you have trouble trusting yourself. For example, "I am thin and rich!" may not be true for me, but "I am attractive, and I have many resources to support me" is true, and it's a powerful affirmation.

- Make it simple and easy to remember. Don't let it be a run-on sentence. Short and sweet is the trick so that, even if you're stressed, you can recall it easily.

Here are some suggestions:

- I find personal growth in discomfort.
- I am calm.
- This discomfort will pass.
- Challenge promotes growth.
- Setting this boundary is healthy and positive.
- I am a (insert Bold Badass archetype here).
- I have control over my thoughts and actions.
- Their opinion is irrelevant.
- I trust my assessment/intuition.

CONSCIOUS BREATHING

When your IDM is on overdrive, taking some time for conscious breathing can help a lot. According to the American Institute of Stress, deep breathing increases the supply of oxygen to your brain and stimulates the parasympathetic nervous system (aka the part of our brain that calms us down).[37]

According to Gina Razón, functional voice coach and former opera singer, young girls (and children of all genders) are often expected to keep quiet and stay still. She says we teach ourselves to do that by engaging the fear response (fight, flight, freeze) and holding our breath.[38] As adults, many of us are still engaged in that breathing pattern, holding our breath when we're nervous or using disordered breathing patterns such as shallow breathing all the time. By disrupting this pattern and being conscious with our breathing, we can remain calm regardless of the situation or our emotional state.

TAKE ACTION: CREATE PERSONAL AFFIRMATIONS

Write out three to five affirmations that you can use to center yourself when anxiety and discomfort have become too much for you. Write them on index cards or in a notes file in your phone. Whenever your Inner Doomsday Machine kicks on, grab your affirmations, and repeat them slowly and with intention at least five times each.

TAKE ACTION: TAKE A DEEP BREATH

Spend a week paying attention to how you breathe in a variety of circumstances. Do you tend to hold your breath when you're nervous or angry? Is your breathing shallow when you're uncertain? Once you've identified your unhealthy breathing patterns, it's time to start turning them around. Focus on your breathing, and when you notice it's not regular and deep, pause to reset. For extra help, find an app that helps you learn to be more conscious with your breathing (I'm a fan of Headspace).

CHAPTER 11

Who's Got Your Back?

TO PARAPHRASE ENGLISH POET JOHN Donne, no woman is an island. It's human nature to need others in your life, so in the next few chapters we're going to talk about who you currently have in your network. Then we'll talk about how to cut out the toxic people in your life so you can focus on how to build a stronger, better network.

At the start of each of my Meetup meetings, I ask what brought the women to the group. We all have a thousand things we could be doing with our time at any given moment, So what makes these women actually come and show up for a meeting called *Ditch the Bitch Stigma*?

About 95 percent of the women over the last few years have said some version of, "I'm looking for women friends who are strong and who appreciate my strength."

There is a real deficit in a lot of women's lives for supportive women friends.

Why Support Matters

It's tough to embrace your inner badass—whatever that looks like to you—all by yourself. When it comes down to it, there are folks around you who don't *want* you to get stronger or be a more direct communicator. Either, because it will hamper their ability to get what they want from you or, because it will remind them that they could make a change too. As you know, the criticisms you'll face are often rooted in the criticizer's own internal fears—and those fears are held to a certain standard that we measure ourselves against. Yet they can still feel personal and demoralizing. This is why it's so important to build a support system for yourself in these new explorations.

Humans are naturally social creatures. We create chosen families and inner circles, and we have a deep-seated desire to be accepted. That's natural. But your current support system may not be supportive of the changes you're making in your life.

If that's the case, there's a two-pronged way to address the issue.

First, take a look at what your relationships with women are currently like. Are they toxic? Do you need to look at cutting them out of your life? As I mentioned earlier, there will be sacrifices along your journey. You will shed certain aspects of your life, including certain relationships, as you learn how to be true to yourself and how to use your voice. There will be people who will feel threatened by that and who will discourage you from growing and evolving in this way. I encourage you to look at those relationships to see if they're draining you and taking time away from developing new, more fulfilling relationships.

That's one of the biggest messages in this book: Don't tolerate someone preventing you from living your fullest life.

If someone is interested in keeping you down or silencing you, you need to understand that it has everything to do with their own life and nothing to do with you. Don't tolerate people who keep you trapped.

The second step in addressing your support system is to get clear on the kinds of relationships you're looking for and to actively look for friend groups that meet those criteria. The women who come to my meetup are looking for friends, and we talk a lot about how difficult it can be to make friends as we get older.

Once we're out of school, we don't have the same environmental triggers as most of our friends, and it's very easy to get sucked into work. We don't always want to build personal relationships with our work colleagues, so we have to proactively look for environments where we're going to find women who will appreciate our evolutions and the new ways we're moving through the world. Don't tolerate less than.

Mutual Admiration Society: Building a Support System

Create a Mutual Admiration Society (MAS) with a group of friends. This should be a network of women—or even just one or two women—who you can reach out to when you are celebrating, when you need a pep talk, or when you need an outside perspective.

These are friends who can give you an unbiased, clear, and honest response to your concerns and help you check your behavior and your progress—and for whom you can do the same. You have to allow each other to be truthful, even if what one of you has to say will be difficult for the other to hear. You don't want to be mean to each other—this is the admiration and support club, and there's no place for toxic femininity—but you do want to be able to be honest so that you can each help each other become stronger and better.

The folks in your Mutual Admiration Society should be people you can trust to encourage you, call you out on your shit, and help you call out others on their shit. The people in your MAS need to be able to do the following:

- Listen to you vent so you can work through your frustration before you talk to the person you're having an issue with

- Reflect back to you what they hear you saying in order to see if you're communicating clearly

- Give you a compassionate critique of your behaviors or responses to tough situations

If you say, "Okay, so here's the situation...was I being rude?" you know your MAS will respond honestly. They may tell you you were really inappropriate and you totally mishandled that situation, then help you figure out how to make amends or solve the problem. Or they may say, "No. You were amazing, and you said exactly what you needed to. Good job." Either way, you know they're speaking honestly and with your best interests at heart. They set you straight when you need it, and they give you support and positive reinforcement when you need that.

They can also be helpful allies when you're combating your Inner Doomsday Machine. Do you feel that negative self-talk or discomfort creeping in? Reach out to your MAS to help you drown out that voice.

Amplification at Work

*"There is a special place in hell for women
who don't help other women."*

—MADELEINE ALBRIGHT, FORMER UNITED STATES
SECRETARY OF STATE

Your MAS can be made up of people from work or your personal life, but I suggest you build an allyship with at least one person at work so that you can be each other's in-office MAS. A lot of women have a much easier time sticking up for someone else than they do for themselves (which is one reason the Advocate profile is one of the most common). When we see an injustice being done to someone else, suddenly our fire kicks in. Find an ally—it doesn't have to be another woman—so that you can boost each other when needed.

This kind of boosting is often called "amplification." It's a concept that was brought to the mainstream discourse when women on President Obama's staff shared how they amplified each other's voices in order to avoid being seen as "self promotional."[39] (In Jessica Bennett's book, *Feminist Fight Club,* she calls it being "boast bitches," which is a fabulous name if you ask me!)[40]

For example, when one of you is being talked over at work, the other one can say something along the lines of, "Regina is making a really good point. Let's focus on that for a moment before we move on."

When someone tries to take credit for your ideas, your ally can say, "Delores was just saying that! Delores, I'd love to hear you elaborate. John, I'd love to hear Delores finish her sentence." If somebody steps on your toes, Delores can do the same for you.

At least at first, it will be easier for you and your allies to advocate for one another than it would for any of us to advocate for ourselves, which can trigger those feelings of selfishness.

Building a Mutual Admiration Society is one of the most fulfilling ways to be successful without trying to change who you are overnight or having to suddenly embody entirely new techniques.

GO DEEPER: ASSESSING YOUR NETWORK

You may not currently have a Mutual Admiration Society, and that's okay. This exercise will help you identify ways to build your network and strengthen your relationships.

The first thing we need to do is take a look at your current network.

Make a list of supportive people in your life. (Sometimes we overlook encouraging people in our lives, so take some time with this one.)

- Which of these people will be particularly supportive of the changes you are making? Reach out to them to discuss your plans.

- Is there someone you've lost touch with who would be great for the new direction you're heading? Reach out to catch up.

- Is there someone you interact with who is not currently in your network, but whom you admire and would like to add? Reach out to get to know them better.

How to Cut Out Toxic People

"No person is your friend who demands your silence or denies your right to grow."

—ALICE WALKER, AUTHOR

In addition to building your Mutual Admiration Society, you may need to cut people out of your network because they can't or won't support you in becoming the person you want to be.

Don't forget that toxic people often view healthy boundaries as abusive.

It's easy to keep people in our lives simply because they have always been there, and even when relationships have run their course, there is pain associated with losing people who are important to us. But if you're already experiencing pain because of the nature of an existing relationship, then ending it is more like ripping off a bandaid. It will hurt, but then you will move forward. I still mourn relationships that I've lost over boundaries I've had to set. However, the way that those people made me feel when they were in my life was worse than how I felt once I left them behind.

Ghosting is a passive-aggressive way of ending a relationship by quietly drifting away and then disappearing altogether, neither offering an explanation nor responding to any messages. By simply avoiding a situation, it can certainly make it easier, and sometimes that's the best option if a confrontation or discussion is likely to make things worse or compromise your safety. If you simply stop reaching out to someone or responding to their outreach, then the relationship might naturally dissolve without having to talk about how you feel.

However, whenever possible, I'm a fan of engaging in direct communication that comes from a place of compassion. I don't ever want to ghost people I might have to cut from my network, and I don't generally advocate you do either. Instead, take some time to sit down and talk. You may find that the relationship is worth preserving.

"Hey, Suzanne, I really wanted to talk to you about this friction that I'm feeling. I feel like there is some pretty intense judgment about me sticking up for myself or speaking clearly about my needs. I just wanted to talk to you about what that might be bringing up for you, or why you think that that's such a negative thing for me to be doing."

Don't come into it with the attitude of, "Well, *you're* acting like a bitch. Why are you judging me?" Remind yourself to consider whether she's legitimately being toxic or you're judging her based on the deeply entrenched Bitch Stigma. Instead of being defensive, come from a place of curiosity and ask for the gift of information. When you come to the conversation with a more compassionately curious perspective, you have a better chance at getting an honest response from the other person. If she's immediately on the defensive, the conversation is over before it can begin. But if she can say something along the lines of, "It makes me uncomfortable when you ask for what you need," that gives you an opportunity to ask whether you can support her in similar efforts. It opens an opportunity for conversation.

The same is true when I think my behavior might have prickled someone else. I was concerned I'd steamrolled a friend recently, so I asked about it directly: "Hey, Megara, I feel like I was talking a lot last time I saw you, and I want to make sure that there's space for you to share." If she felt fine, that's great. But if she did feel like I'd bulldozed her, I wanted her to be able to tell me. That way we could both take responsibility for ourselves.

Take some time before you start sitting down with these people and work through the conversation with another friend who doesn't have any skin in the game. In this safe space, you'll be able to express all your feelings however you need to—even if that's level-ten bitchy—without worrying about hurting the other relationship. Once you've worked through those raw feelings, you'll be able to take a more calm stance in the actual conversation.

I have lost friendships with people who didn't appreciate that style, but those friendships then weren't giving me what I needed. I have absolutely had friends reject me when I came to them with compassionate care. It's not easy, but when I bring up a behavior that's hurting me, and they don't want to hear it, that's a sign to me that we can't honestly communicate, and this isn't a relationship that I should prioritize. But the only way to find out is by giving it a shot.

Think about a time that someone said something rude to you. It might have been a colleague or a friend or family member. They say something that is rude and hurtful, but they do it in the "just kidding, LOL" sort of way. Imagine being able to stand up for yourself in that moment with a firm response. Imagine that, rather than absorbing the negativity and the hurt, you can let it bounce off you and fall to the floor.

This is what happens when you let go of the Bitch Stigma.

GO DEEPER: IS THIS RELATIONSHIP TOXIC?

Have you ever had to discontinue a friendship? What happened? Are you happy with how you handled the situation?

Here are some questions to ask yourself when you're trying to determine if a friend is toxic and whether you need to move on.

- Are they overly competitive with you? When you share good news or progress you've made in your personal or professional life, do they immediately shift the attention back to themselves or respond negatively to what you're saying?

- Are you the one who's always reaching out or organizing times to hang out? Do they seem far less invested in the relationship than you are?

- Do you feel like you have to walk on eggshells around them? Are they prone to lashing out when they're upset or frustrated?

- Do they refuse to apologize when they've genuinely done something damaging to you or to your relationship?

- Do you feel stress, anxiety, or mistrust when you're interacting with them?

Building Your Network

As we get older it can feel harder to find new friends and create new connections. But it is possible, and that means that your network isn't restricted to people you already know. Often, our networks are made up of relationships of convenience; family, neighbors, childhood friends, work friends, etc. These connections may be perfectly healthy, but they may not be built on shared values such as the desire to better yourself.

Once you've shored up your network by assessing who you want to keep and cutting toxic relationships, it's time to take control of who you allow in your life and start seeking out people who share your values and ambitions. This takes effort: new relationships don't just spring up overnight. But the payoff is more than worth the investment. You need to seek out the kinds of people who will help you move forward in your life.

GROUPS TO JOIN

We live in the internet age where it's imminently possible to find folks. Granted, you might have to kiss a lot of frogs, but the first thing to do is to look in the right places.

Use sites like Meetup.com and introduce yourself to people who seem outgoing and confident. Actively work to get to know the people you meet and admire, showing up as consistently as you can in the most impactful ways you can.

You can also join professional organizations or political/activist organizations in order to meet people in the same industry or with similar beliefs. These days, there are multiple weekend events catering to women looking to build friendships and empowerment.

Since you get to build this new section of your friendship network from the ground up, you can also look for specific traits that will contribute strength to your MAS.

In 2013, Ann Friedman wrote an article for *The Cut* that coined the phrase "Shine Theory."[41] This refers to the idea that "powerful women make the greatest friends." The "Shine Theory" touches on the competition that women can feel, which can cause us to shy away from befriending a woman who "shines" with self confidence from fear that we'll look worse by comparison. In reality, that friend can boost your confidence, because self-confidence is infectious, and your fabulous friend won't let you feel anything but amazing about yourself. When you surround yourself with powerful, supportive women it adds to your own strength.

Here are a few of the kinds of traits to look for in new members of your MAS:

- They're truth-tellers and straight-shooters. We may not always want to hear the truth, but we need someone in our life to tell it to us.

- They are strong communicators.

- They're trustworthy and aren't going to share your thoughts and experiences with other people.

- They're willing and able to invest time and energy into their relationships. They answer the phone when you call and respond when you text.

- Once you meet those people, you also need to invest time and energy into creating a connection. You have to work to cultivate connection. It takes effort, but the effort is worth it.

According to friendship expert Shasta Nelson, author of *Frientimacy and Friendships Don't Just Happen!* (a book I highly recommend), there are three requirements of healthy friendships.[42]

1. Positivity: The friend makes you feel positive and approaches the friendship with positivity rather than spending the whole-time whining. Friendship is about two people raising the emotional happiness of each other.

2. Consistency: Friendships grow and deepen based on the history you've built and the time you spend together. It's impossible to build a healthy relationship if you don't spend actual time connecting. It's the repetition or regularity that develops patterns, rituals, and expectations in our relationships.

3. Vulnerability: This is the "real talk" of sharing your insecurities and your dreams, and the security to be able to ask for what you need from your friends and to feel known. It's allowing someone else to hear your ideas, know your opinions, validate your feelings, and listen to your experiences.

This can be another useful time to break out the Mirror Matrix. Take special note of the archetypes you don't currently embody and those that would be helpful to surround yourself with. Are you more of a Queen, keeping your thoughts to yourself most of the time? Would it be helpful to be friends with a Rebel so that you learn how to speak up more often? Or maybe you're a Rogue who needs an Advocate in your life to help you see how diplomacy works.

Be careful in how you cultivate these relationships. You don't have to rely on connections of convenience. Go out and seek the kind of women you want to be friends with and build yourself a badass Mutual Admiration Society.

GO DEEPER: HOW WILL YOU BUILD YOUR NETWORK?

- Make a list of places and ways you can look for new people to be part of your Mutual Admiration Society.

- How can you make time to meet new people?

- How can you make time and space for new friends?

Want to reach out to friends but don't know what to say? Get a cheat sheet with a handful of messages you can use at Bitch-Stigma.com/library

SECTION 4

BECOMING THE BITCH

NOW IT'S TIME TO DIVE deep and turn all these theories into actions. This is when I'm going to lean into my background to give you even more strategies for embracing your inner badass. The techniques in this chapter have helped me—and in turn, my clients—create core confidence and a reliable persona of strength and authority, which I call my "Most Confident Self." These strategies have empowered me to create a very successful career as a professional bitch, and they're the same techniques I've used for years with my coaching clients to give them a source of badassery to draw on anytime, anywhere.

Are you ready?

In the next few chapters we're going to focus on how to take action to live life your way. You may be starting from scratch, or you might already be pretty satisfied with your inner badass and just looking to up your game. Either way, by the end of this section, you're going to have a full profile of your Most Confident Self, highlighting your current strengths alongside ways to bolster your confidence skills. You'll learn what it takes to embody your Most Confident Self and access your power anytime you choose.

Here we go!

"Find out who you are and do it on purpose."

—DOLLY PARTON, SINGER-SONGWRITER

CHAPTER 12

Building Confidence

I'VE MENTIONED THAT, LIKE MANY women, I was raised to be polite and not rock the boat. Above all, I was to be selfless—never self-centered. But when I entered the BDSM world, I had to learn how to overcome those ingrained expectations to discover and embrace my "dominant self."

I started with a name: Princess Kali. Maybe Kali Williams wasn't supposed to be self-centered, but Princess Kali sure as hell was. She got to be self-centered and *celebrated for it.*

Of course, it wasn't easy, so to help reinforce the new persona behind the new name, I wore an actual tiara. As I was learning to express my confidence in this new way, I'd remind myself that, as long as the tiara was on my head, I was allowed to be self-centered. In fact, my being self-centered was positive and desired.

After I'd practiced this way for a while, it became like muscle memory. I would put the tiara on, and then suddenly powerful Kali would come out swinging. "Yeah, I'm in charge. I'm the one dictating everything. You have to listen to me and focus on me." But I only had to be in charge of everything for an hour. Then I could take the tiara off. For years, I never went anywhere work-related without the tiara, because it helped me embody my most confident self. (And it had become a big part of my brand.) Today I don't need the tiara. It was a spark for me early on, but now I've internalized that feeling of power and I can access it on my own.

Needless to say, I'm a big believer in tiaras, but it can be any accessory that makes you feel like the Bold Badass you are. Whatever your "tiara" is, wear it when you're doing the dishes, wear it when you are practicing your big speech. Wear *something* that will give you a sense of your own power.

Sensory Sparks

The tiara is an example of what I call a "Sensory Spark." These are ways to use your senses to reinforce confidence. Our senses are an incredibly powerful influence on our internal state. The smell of apple pie may bring up a certain memory for you. I grew up in the country and lived by a dairy farm, so weirdly enough, the smell of manure is very nostalgic for me. But it's not just about nostalgia. We can use Sensory Sparks to create shortcuts to our most badass, confident selves. Using our senses can help us get into our subconscious to override social training.

Sensory Sparks are a kind of Pavlovian conditioning.[43] Our sense memory can spark an emotional state quickly and easily, and we can use that to our advantage when looking to create our own confidence stimulus. One of the more fun techniques that I recommend is to find some sort of Sensory Spark you can use when you are already feeling confident.

For example, a woman I coached had lost a lot of her confidence as she aged and went through several difficult life events.

We found a perfume that she had worn frequently during the times when she'd felt glorious and powerful. There was already a sense memory attached to that perfume, so I had her put it on when she was already feeling confident (when she closed a sale or when she flirted with someone and they flirted back) to reinforce that memory and that feeling. That way, when she faced a situation where she struggled to tap into her confidence, she could apply that perfume and her brain would respond to the conditioned stimulus and remind her what confidence feels like.

I use this technique myself with bergamot essential oil. When I'm feeling powerful, I smell the oil to build that mental association between the bergamot scent and the feeling of power and confidence. **Now my mind knows that when I'm feeling badass, there's bergamot in the air. And conversely, when there's bergamot in the air, I feel like a badass.** So when I'm heading into a situation where I know I'll need a boost, I can apply just a touch of my bergamot essential oil, and I'll be smelling—and more importantly, feeling—confident all day.

And it's not just smell. I have a friend who puts a couple flakes of sea salt in her mouth when she needs to feel "salty." When she's feeling salty, she has the confidence to speak her mind. I know of another woman who wears a leather garter under her "soccer mom" clothes on the days when she needs to tap into her Rebel self.

Another common Sensory Spark is finding a "power song" or album that you can listen to to get yourself pumped up and in the mood. Music has a major effect on our mood. I'm sure you know that feeling when one of your favorite songs comes on and you can't help but sit up straighter and tap your feet or even get up to boogie.

Another way to build confidence is to become more aware of your body and to use your body language consciously.

Getting into your body can be an excellent Sensory Spark, because when your body feels strong, it's easier to feel confident. No matter what your body shape, size, or ability, it can be helpful to get out of your head and into your body, whatever that might mean for you.

When it comes to body language, there are a few key moves you can use to boost your sense of empowerment. The way we carry ourselves physically can have a big impact on how we feel psychologically and on how others perceive us. When I coach women to discover their sexual dominance, one of the main things we work on is paying more attention to the way they move in order to fully physically embody their power.

So when you need to find your confidence, stretch, or dance if you can. Don't just walk—strut.

POWER POSES

Around 2012, Amy Cuddy's take on the science behind power posing became popular.[44] I saw her present at SXSW in 2014 and was exhilarated to see her sharing scientific research to support the idea that the way you stand and move can change the way you feel and the way others feel about you. The way I naturally stand (feet planted firmly, hands on my hips) has always been noted as one of the things that makes me "intimidating," but I believe that this pose (known as the Wonder Woman pose) is an easy way to look and feel self-assured.

After Amy Cuddy's talk, I went up to thank her. When I mentioned that I had experienced a lot of what she was talking about as a professional dominatrix, she laughed and said, "That's one of the few places women can express their power openly!"

Her response was fantastic, and she was right. My natural "Wonder Woman" stance was put to very good use as a dominatrix, where my easy authority was appreciated. Another power pose I used frequently was to stand tall over a kneeling man with my finger pointed and a twinkle in my eye. When I coach women to embrace their sexual empowerment, one of the first things we work on is helping them find the power poses that help them feel a sense of ownership over their own bodies.

Another perfect example of a power pose is Megan Rapinoe's stance throughout the 2019 World Cup and after their win.[45] She stands with her legs solidly together, back straight, chin up, arms stretched out in a clear declaration of her triumph. That kind of power, unabashedly expressed with her whole energy and physical being, is exactly the embodiment of badassery we're looking for.

The most obvious—but often most difficult—power pose is one we should be using all day, every day: Stand up straight! With as much time as we all spend on the computer or watching TV or hunched over our phones, it's easy to be a sloucher (I have to fight the tendency all the time). But when you roll your shoulders back and keep your head up, you'll look and feel much more confident. The more practiced we are at carrying ourselves like badasses, the easier it will be to channel Megan Rapinoe and stand up tall in the face of any stigma.

ENGAGING YOUR SENSES

As we've seen, using taste, scent, sight, sound, touch, movement, or even wearing a special necklace or item of clothing, allows us to tap into sense memories of our most confident moments and summon some of that confidence for our present situations.

So find something—a scent, taste, item, or movement—that you associate with being in a powerful headspace. Keep it handy, and you'll always have a shortcut to confidence.

Another kind of Sensory Spark technique I love to use and teach is a little more internal, but it's no less powerful. Sit quietly and either remember a time that you were confident or imagine a situation in which you would be confident and try to picture as many details as possible. Think firmly about that scenario, whether it's a memory or from your imagination, and try to get it into your body. Once you are in that mindset—once you're fully inhabiting your body—*then* apply the external Sensory Spark. Taste the honey, apply the perfume, or put on your power pantsuit.

Over the last twenty years, this has been one of the most powerfully life-changing techniques my coaching clients have used. The Sensory Spark is just a shortcut to a confidence boost, and that's a completely natural thing to need. But this technique only works if you practice it consistently. You've got to invest the time to pay attention to when you are feeling confident or empowered and then remember to associate that sense with your spark. Just like practicing direct language in a safe space, structure supports spontaneity with Sensory Sparks as well. If you constantly reinforce your most confident moments with your Sensory Spark, you'll be ready to call on it at a moment's notice.

You might feel silly the first few times, but I guarantee that if you stick with it, it will be transformative.

TAKE ACTION: TAP INTO YOUR SENSORY SPARKS

What are your strongest senses to tap into as Sensory Sparks? Make a list of each sense and what you might be able to use as a Sensory Spark. Once you have a small list for each sense, circle the ones that will be the most powerful.

Here are some examples of Sensory Sparks you can use:

- Taste (honey, chocolate, salt, wine, tea)
- Sight (looking at a candle or photo)

- Touch (item to wear or stroke, such as a tiara, shoes, clothing, a stone)
- Smell (perfume/cologne, essential oil)
- Sound (song, album, gong, soundscapes)
- Movement (yoga, power pose, a special dance step)

For the next week, whenever you feel confident and strong, use your Sensory Spark. Always keep it handy with you. Use the Sensory Spark *every* time you have a moment of confidence, and soon you'll be able to use that spark to summon confidence, too.

Role-play Characteristics, Not Characters

Role-play is a common tool in the kink world, and it's been one of my most successful crossover techniques for my coaching clients, regardless of what kind of confidence boost they're seeking.

Role-play is when you "play" with new concepts based on roles you are choosing to embody. These roles can be amplifications of a part of yourself, or they can be entirely concocted personas. There are plenty of stereotypes about role-play. Some might think of the LARP community (Live Action Role-Playing) that dresses in elaborate costumes for play acting battles. Or it might call to mind the classic naughty nurse and eager patient bedroom play. Both of those can be very fun, but I'm suggesting something different.

TO BUILD CONFIDENCE, ROLE-PLAY *CHARACTERISTICS*, NOT *CHARACTERS*.

What do I mean by that?

Let's take a classic role-play character: the cowboy. On one hand, you can put on a cowboy hat, but you're still the same person: you, in a cowboy hat. My goal is to help you think about the characteristics that we associate with cowboys. Cowboys have swagger, they're practical and direct. They might have a rough-and-tumble approach. Maybe they smolder, or are more of a corn-fed, open-hearted type. They use few words to communicate. These are the *characteristics* that make up a *character*.

For another example, I worked with a couple in which the woman played the dominant role in the relationship but was very soft-spoken and a bit passive in her everyday life. She had a very difficult time being assertive, let alone being demanding as the dominant both she and her partner desired her to be. We figured out that for her to feel comfortable being demanding, she had to role-play that she was someone else.

When we get told our entire lives—by others as well as ourselves— who we are and how we are in the world, it can be tough to break free of those stereotypes. Has anybody ever said to you, "You're never going to want to do that. I know how you are."

We get this picture of ourselves, and sometimes in order to get out from underneath that, we have to pretend to be someone we're not with characteristics that aren't yet authentic for us. We get trapped in the role that we think we're supposed to play, and that makes it hard to do certain activities. But when we "become" someone else, we can explore new boundaries—we can fake it till we are it.

"If you know what you think about yourself, you're going to care a lot less about what other people think about you."

—JANET HARDY, WRITER AND SEX EDUCATOR

Have you ever read about Beyoncé's alter ego, Sasha Fierce? In an interview with Oprah, she said she crafted her stage persona to help her overcome challenges and give the best performances she can. "It's kind of like doing a movie. When you put on the wig and put on the clothes, you walk different," she says.[46]

We learn to role-play early in our lives in order to please others. It's natural to act differently depending on who we're with and what the situation is. Now it's time to turn this back to *our* advantage rather than using it to make others comfortable.

Just like the other confidence-building activities we've discussed, in role-play, success begets success. The more you do it the more comfortable you become with it. The better it gets, the more fun it is, the more you want to do it, and the better you get at it, it's a self-confirming cycle. This is also a big reason why practicing and role-playing situations with friends is so helpful— it's a low-risk chance to practice embodying the traits we're striving for. For extra practice, improv classes are fairly affordable and easy to come by, and can go a long way in helping you learn to think on your feet and inhabit different selves. The better you get at role-playing Bold Badass behaviors, the more you'll find you feel confident setting boundaries, shutting down bad behavior, or navigating situations that have traditionally been uncomfortable.

TIPS FOR ROLE-PLAY:

- Get over feeling silly and give it all you've got. Role-play isn't effective if you don't let go of your self-judgement and sincerely play along.

- When you're role-playing for practice, create the bubble! This is what I call it when you agree with your partner that you're going to make your own rules, support each other, and laugh together without judgment.

- Inhabit the role-play as much as possible. Use clothes, shoes, movement, and more to really get into your new persona.

- You can role-play as either a persona completely different from your own, or you can simply work on accessing and expressing a special part of your-self. Find the characteristics in the role that you relate to or can imagine yourself playing and try to relax into it.

- Use your imagination (and maybe a few well-placed props) to turn your environment into the situation you need to make your role-play successful. Use ver-bal cues to describe the "place" you are in as that helps craft the psychological aspect of role-play as practice for "the real thing."

CHAPTER 13

Structure Supports Spontaneity

WHEN IT COMES TO BEING clever or witty or sexy or empowered, there's an unrealistic expectation that it will just "come to you" in the moment and that if it doesn't come to you, you must not be witty or sexy or empowered. But here's the good news: that's not usually how it works. Very few people are simply born with that talent. Like anything, we learn to be spontaneous by studying, practicing, and preparing. By planning ahead and using a structure to prepare, we can be more ready for successful spontaneous responses. One of my most frequent sayings in my workshops is "structure supports spontaneity."

This kind of groundwork boosts confidence because it means we never have to feel like we're walking into a situation unprepared. When we let go of the expectation that we'll just naturally know what to say when someone is challenging us, then we can develop techniques that let us feel ready for any situation.

"Power is not given to you. You have to take it."

—BEYONCÉ, SINGER-SONGWRITER

There are multiple ways to put this saying into effect, but the most important one is by practicing, individually and with friends.

Practice in Action

You've spent a lifetime building up your coping mechanisms and self-defeating behaviors, so it's going to take a little time to retrain yourself to behave differently than you have for twenty, thirty or forty years. But practice will help you speed up the process. At the beginning of the section I talked about having friends to practice with, and your Mutual Admiration Society are exactly what I was talking about. This is a good time to tell them about this book (if you haven't already) and set up a time to practice the upcoming techniques together.

Find a friend you're comfortable with, get together to have a cup of tea or a glass of wine, and practice interrupting each other. Or say to your extroverted friend, "I'm trying to get more comfortable speaking up for myself, so I might interrupt you a couple of times while we're hanging out today, or over the next couple weeks. This is why...."

More often than not, your friends will get on board. Present your experiment as personal growth, help them understand what you're doing, and get them on your team.

Putting yourself in an environment where other women are encouraging this new behavior will allow you to feel more confident doing it. Because even if you aren't getting the responses you want in the "real world" right away, you'll have someone—your ally at work or your practice buddy—telling you that you're doing the right thing. It can be exceptionally powerful to feel like somebody has got your back in that way.

And I guarantee the more that you practice empowerment in safe spaces, the stronger the sense memory will be when you're in a higher energy, higher stakes situation.

We've all heard the phrase "Practice Makes Perfect," but I want to adapt it to "Practice Makes Proficient" because perfection is not what we're looking for. By using practice to make ourselves more comfortable, we become more proficient in speaking up, even in imperfect ways.

Practicing will help you in three significant ways:

1. You'll build confidence by working through scenarios ahead of time.

2. You'll improve your reflexes so that, when a "real-life" situation comes up, you won't need as much time to process what's happening and you'll be able to respond immediately.

3. You literally change your brain.

What are you practicing, exactly? Any scenario where you feel like you could use extra confidence. Maybe you felt like you got walked all over at work last week, and you want to figure out how to handle it better next time. Or maybe you have a tough conversation coming up with a romantic partner, and you want to practice expressing your needs clearly and rationally. The beauty of practice is that you can tailor it to fit your exact needs.

Actors practice developing sense memory to create a kind of "emotional recall," and it's useful for us as well. Brian Timoney, an acting coach, describes it as "manipulating your own experiences to create a truthful emotional performance."[47] Until you fully integrate your ideal traits, combining sense memory with role-play during practice will help you develop an inner wellspring of confidence that you can draw on whenever you need it.

If you don't have the sense memory of how to respond and if you don't have that natural tendency to set firm boundaries (which is likely the whole reason you're reading this book), you may not have those tools. It's easy to get into the habit of waiting for something that is "big enough" or "horrible enough" to start building this skill. But if you don't start by curbing the little things like innocuous interruptions or incorrect restaurant orders—the things that are easier to endure or ignore rather than cause a fuss about—then you won't be well-practiced when it comes to the big things like your career, your safety, or your emotional needs.

When you're trying to imagine being more confident it may seem silly to think about something as small as ordering your food exactly how you want it and sending it back if it's not correct, but you have to start somewhere. For some women there is strength in this small gesture.

The only way you can really get comfortable setting boundaries or using you new tools in high-stakes moments is by practicing them in no-pressure or low pressure situations, because that's how you can train your body and your mind to respond in new ways rather than falling back into your old style.

Try out your new role-playing skills, fire up your Sensory Sparks, and practice this with a friend or with a couple of friends. That's what creates a support system to encourage you when you are in the midst of this difficult transition or having to deal with how others adapt to your new approach. You'll need some consistent affirmation, and who better to provide it than the people you practice with.

You're trying to counteract a lifetime of socialization that says: sit down, shut up, and smile. Be pleasant, be a team player, don't make waves. Don't be difficult. It's going to take practice to overcome those trained behaviours and develop new reflexive responses. Having a team of people who are encouraging you, who are practicing with you, who are part of the process in a positive way, is going to give you a safe space to retreat to when things are difficult.

"She was unstoppable. Not because she did not have failures or doubts, but because she continued on despite them."

— BEAU TAPLIN, AUTHOR

There are moments in your life when you feel like the strongest version of yourself. Now, that version may not be as strong as you want yet, but it's a good place to start, so think about what those moments might be. It might be when you take your dog for a walk and he listens to you. It might be finding an error in your team's work product just in time to fix it before it goes to a client. You don't have to be able to pinpoint some big circus-show example of confidence. Even the smallest instances can be seed to grow from.

TAKE ACTION: FIELD RESEARCH

Start by spending a week paying attention to how many times you or women around you acquiesce to make others comfortable. Make a note of every single time you see a woman agree to something she's obviously not happy with or accept something she obviously doesn't want.

After a week of keeping track of these incidents, go back through and write how that woman (or you) could've responded differently. What are the words that could've been said instead?

Once you start seeing all the ways women stifle ourselves, it's impossible to unsee.

TAKE ACTION: PRACTICE BEING A BADASS

Once you've become used to paying attention, at least twice a week, for the next three weeks, choose low or no-pressure situations where you can practice. Put on your "tiara" (whatever that is for you) and practice feeling like a badass. Stop a good friend when she accidentally interrupts you at lunch. Role-play a heated conversation with a colleague to work out the best way to stand your ground. After each session, write down or record a few thoughts about how it felt to test out your new confidence tools.

Affirmations

We talked about affirmations when we looked at how to shut off the Inner Doomsday Machine, but that's not all they're good for. When it comes to building confidence, affirmations can be an incredibly useful tool, especially when we use them in a structured way. Just like the same Sensory Spark won't work for every woman, neither will the same affirmations.

Below are several suggested affirmations for building confidence, based on each Bold Badass archetype. (Of course, you're not limited to the affirmations associated with your primary archetype. You can also create your own or borrow from situational or aspirational archetypes at any time!)

Archetypes in Action

ADVOCATE AFFIRMATIONS

What I fight for is righteous; I am a champion for others.
I build a habit of speaking up for myself.
Confidence is strength.
My voice is my power.

WARRIOR AFFIRMATIONS

I command respect.
My convictions are worth sticking up for.
My principles are more important than others' comfort.
I am fierce, and that is good.

QUEEN AFFIRMATIONS

It's okay to be quiet.
Direct communication is effective communication.
My dignity is my strength.
I weigh my words before speaking.

BOSS AFFIRMATIONS

I have earned the respect that I expect.
My skills are useful and important and deserve to be valued.
My high standards are what get things done.
I embrace my leadership position.

REBEL AFFIRMATIONS

I blaze my own trail.
Big things happen outside the box.
I'm bold and outspoken. I'm fierce and fearless.
My actions create my successes.

ROGUE AFFIRMATIONS

My sense of self is formidable.
I am a force of nature.
My intensity is unapologetic.
I don't speak, I roar.

DAILY JOURNALING

A really great way to track your progress is through daily journaling to record your thoughts, feelings, and experiences as you work to embrace your inner badass. Setting your thoughts and actions down on paper makes them more tangible. Don't worry, you don't need to spend a ton of time each day on this, but even writing just a sentence or three down at the start of the day to set your intentions—and/or at the end of the day to document your actions—will help you see faster, deeper, and more trackable progress.

For help getting started, visit BitchStigma.com/Journal

GO DEEPER: HOW DO YOU SPEAK UP AND SET BOUNDARIES?

- What did you do today to set your verbal boundaries?

- What did you do today to set your physical boundaries?

- Did you need to use situational or aspirational archetypes today? What happened?

- Was there a time that you wanted to speak up but didn't? If so, describe what happened and what you'd like to do differently next time.

Rewarding Yourself: The Gold Star System

Let's talk a little bit about motivation. Making change can be difficult, and it's important to find inspiration to stay committed even when the change is taking time.

Intrinsic motivation describes behaviors that are driven by internal rewards. This is when we feel proud for doing the right thing even if nothing tangible comes of it. We commit to a behavior because it's internally satisfying.

Extrinsic motivation refers to when the motivation for a behavior comes from wanting to earn a reward or avoid punishment.

While many folks think that intrinsic motivation is the ideal, I'm a fan of using extrinsic motivation to get things going. Having something tangible that we enjoy as a reward for exploring difficult behavior gives us something to hold onto until that intrinsic motivation kicks in once we've experienced some progress.

GOLD STAR FOR ADULTING

My mother was a kindergarten teacher for many years, and I'm pretty sure that's influenced me in a major way. I'm a sucker for a gold star, so I've come back around to using them to help me stay motivated even when things are rough.

There are going to be moments when it's hard. Trying these new techniques can be uncomfortable, and it may be easier for us to think, "I'm gonna go back to the old system. I wasn't particularly happy, but at least I knew how to do it."

Though the ultimate reward is the feeling of moving through the world with power and confidence, getting what we need, and having our boundaries respected, the short-term rewards of "gold stars" will help us feel good about the new behaviors—and keep them up—before the long-term rewards are clear. For example, if we give ourselves a self-care-related treat every time we speak out in a difficult situation, we'll start to associate the act with the reward—just like a Sensory Spark.

"In a society that profits from your self-doubt, liking yourself is a rebellious act."

— CAROLINE CALDWELL, ARTIST

Ultimately, our experiences in the world will become healthier and happier once we're being true to ourselves, living life for our own needs, and making sure our voices are heard. It's impossible to move through life with everyone liking us, but our own opinions about ourselves are the only ones that really, truly matter. After all, when we go home every night, its our own reflections we must reckon with. When you look at yourself in the mirror, do you see someone who's authentic, confident, and true to herself? Or someone who's sacrificed her own needs in order to fit in a box made for somebody else?

When we learn that, as women, we can be both respected and generally liked enough, then we're free to believe in our own evaluations of how we're living life. There is a freedom in letting go of letting other people dictate our behavior and imposing limitations on our experiences, including ambition and love and anything else we feel is being squashed by these obstacles.

One day, those feelings will become second nature, and you'll have more intrinsic motivation than you know what to do with. But until then, figure out what kind of gold star will keep you going.

There are a few things to keep in mind when you're building a reward system:

1. It must be truly motivational. If it's something that you'll have anytime (like a candy bar or a talk with a friend), it's not sufficiently motivational to help you get over the hump of not wanting to do it.

2. The reward can't be harmful or counterproductive.

3. It's best if it's something that you can do yourself rather than depending on someone else to provide.

GO DEEPER: INCENTIVIZING CONFIDENCE

- What are you going to do to reward yourself when you change your behavior before you get to the outcome?

- What can you do to continue to keep yourself inspired to work on these changes?

- Make a list of self-care behaviors that you can rely on when the going gets tough.

TAKE ACTION: KEEP TRACK FOR A MONTH

Visit BitchStigma.com/Downloads for a page of "gold stars" to help you keep track of one month of a new habit. Color in each star at the end of the day once you've done the new thing. Or even better, buy a set of inexpensive gold star stickers and use those to acknowledge your daily success. Once you've reached the goal you've set for yourself, reward yourself as planned!

CHAPTER 14

Your Most Confident Self

EVERYTHING YOU'VE READ, PRACTICED, AND reflected on until now has been leading to this moment, when you put all of the techniques together to create your Most Confident Self. Your Most Confident Self profile is a way to be aware, to set intentions, and to remind you of who you are and who you want to be.

Time to break out the archetypes again. This is where they really get fun. Remember the five archetypes I asked you to keep in mind when we first introduced the Mirror Matrix?

Core

Secondary

Aspirational

Situational

Toxic

These are the archetypes that most resonate with you in one way or another. Your core and secondary archetypes are the ones you gravitate to naturally, your aspirational profile is who you want to be, and your situational archetypes are the ones you can lean into as necessary, depending on what's going on around you. Your toxic profile is the archetype you embody when you're not at your best. Don't worry, we all have one of those, but let's put it aside for now and focus on the first four.

These four archetypes make up your "Most Confident Self," and when you embody your MCS (Most Confident Self), you can access and inhabit any of these archetypes when you need them.

Think of this set of archetypes like a confidence wardrobe. As you build your most confident self, consider which pieces are staples (your core and secondary archetypes), which ones are accents (your situational archetypes), and which are bold statement pieces (aspirational archetypes) you'd like to add.

The beauty of the Mirror Matrix and the MCS is that it allows each of us to create and embody authentic confidence. Just like the ideal wardrobe contains pieces that fit us well and are true to our unique styles, the "confidence wardrobe" holds the Bold Badass archetypes that fit each of us individually. Nobody feels good in a confidence suit that doesn't fit.

Finally, remember that as you're building your Most Confident Self, confidence is a journey, *not* a destination! This won't likely be an instant transformation, and there are a lot of factors that influence confidence. It's critical that you're compassionate with yourself throughout the process.

GO DEEPER: ENVISIONING YOUR MOST CONFIDENT SELF

- What does your Most Confident Self look like?
- Think about what your life would be like if the Bitch Stigma wasn't holding you back. What would

you do differently? How would you communicate with others?

- What are the words you want associated with your MCS? How do you want others to perceive you? How do you want to feel inside?

- How will you talk? What are the words you'll use or not use? What does your tone of voice sound like? What style of communication will you choose? How do you use or not use humor?

- How will you move? How does your walking style or stride change? What kind of eye contact do you use? What does your personal space bubble look like? How do you enforce that space?

- Do you dress differently or change your appearance in any way? Are different colors attractive to you? What does the style of your clothing look like?

- How will you interact differently with people in various aspects of your life? Work? Friends? Family? Intimate partners?

Who Inspires You?

When we begin the process of making any changes to our lives—whether we're embracing our inner badass or anything else—it can be immensely helpful to look toward role models, both in our own lives and in pop culture. Think back to the examples in the archetype profiles illustrating the different kinds of bitches and badasses and consider which of these women embody characteristics you envision as part of your MCS.

"It's not your job to like me, it's mine."

—BYRON KATIE, SPEAKER AND AUTHOR

Who are the role models we can look to for examples of the characteristics we strive for? How do we find them? How do we ascertain that they have the characteristics to make an effective, nontoxic role model? Can we see it from afar? Do we have to be in a relationship with someone to really understand their motives and the difference between bad bitchy and good bitchy?

First, we don't have to know someone in person to adopt them as a role model. In fact, it can be helpful to model yourself after somebody you don't know, whether that's a fictional character like Liz Taylor's Cleopatra, who has a calm, commanding demeanor, or a real-life celebrity like Nicki Minaj, who is known for speaking her mind.

Second, no one person has to be the perfect role model. It's okay to aspire to certain aspects of several different people. You may admire one person's rebelliousness, another's passion, and another's quick wit. A role model can be an amalgamation of several powerful women.

Women often think that we have to be strong in a certain way, and if that way doesn't resonate with us, then we're hopeless. But that couldn't be further from the truth. If one model of confidence isn't ideal for you, don't write off the idea altogether. Instead look for the archetypes that do resonate and the role models who embody characteristics that vibe with *your* unique strength.

The options are endless.

TAKE ACTION: IDENTIFY YOUR ROLE MODELS

It's important for women not to feel like we have to fit ourselves into any one archetype. So let's examine some different role models we can look to as inspiration. We can start with the examples listed in each Bold Badass archetype.

Next, make a list of the powerful women who inspire you. You can draw from the archetype profiles or you can brainstorm your own. Underneath each name, write out the traits you want to internalize. List every reason you can think of for why you look up to each person. Now go through and circle the top five or six characteristics that you want to bring into your life.

How can you start to develop these traits in yourself? Think of the Sensory Sparks, role-play opportunities, and practice scenarios that can help you get started.

Most Confident Self Profile

In each of these sections, write why the profile resonated for you:

Core Archetype:

Secondary Archetype:

Aspirational Archetype(s):

Situational Archetype(s):

Sensory Sparks:

Sight:

Scent:

Sound:

Touch:

Taste:

Movement:

Additional Confidence Boosters:

Theme songs:

Body language:

Ideal traits:

Role models:

Affirmations:

TAKE ACTION: BRING YOUR MOST CONFIDENT SELF TO LIFE

CREATE YOUR MCS PROFILE

Start by going to BitchStigma.com/Downloads to get a blank Most Confident Self Plan template, including a blank MCS profile, a place to plan out your Mutual Admiration Society, and some journal prompts to help you track your progress. Spend some time working through the template and personalizing your profile and action plans.

BUILD A VISION BOARD

Now, let's make your MCS even more tangible. You can do this while you're filling out your profile if you need some inspiration, or, after you're done, when you're ready to bring your ideas to life. A vision board is a physical reminder of who you are and who you want to become. It's time to take the brainstorming, writing, and reflecting from our work throughout this book and turn it into a visual blueprint of the self you're celebrating and creating.

Vision boards have become a popular topic of articles and Pinterest pages, but did you know that they really can be beneficial? Though probably not exactly in the way you might think.

Making a vision board can be fun, and especially so if you do it with a group of friends or your MAS. But you can't stop there. Positive thinking is a good place to start, but it's the actionability that makes real change. As *The Little Prince* author Antoine de Saint-Exupéry said, *"A goal without a plan is just a wish."*

There's no way having some motivational quotes and pictures of far-off destinations can inherently make change in your life. But they can be an excellent reminder of why you're taking action to make change. Your vision board is a place of visual inspiration and encouragement.

Science has shown that simply imagining winning or achieving your goals isn't nearly as beneficial as imagining *working to achieve* your goals.[48] When you focus on the feeling you'll have once you're already successful, your unconscious mind wants to count that as success. It's ready to jump to the good stuff and skip right over the working-to-get-there bit. But when you focus on the feeling of *working for it*, that's when your brain starts to associate hard work with good feelings.

Let your vision board represent success, of course, but make sure its primary focus is on the actions you'll take to achieve that success. Your vision board might include pictures of women talking to each other to represent new relationships you're building or friends you need to have hard conversations with. It might include photos that represent challenging situations like team meetings or first dates that you're working to embrace, or some of your affirmations or the Sensory Sparks you're using to help create sense memories of confidence.

The beauty of a vision board is that there aren't any rules about what you can and can't include. Just be sure to focus on the effort you're making, not just the end results you're striving for.

SECTION 5

BITCH IN ACTION

THIS LAST SECTION IS ALL about setting and asserting boundaries. You've been practicing and role-playing, you have a clear vision of your Most Confident Self, and now it's time to jump in the deep end and use your newfound skills and confidence to make some big, bold moves without fear of being labeled a bitch.

CHAPTER 15

Communication Is a Gift

THE FIRST—AND MOST IMPORTANT—THING TO keep in mind when you're setting boundaries is that communication is a gift. I learned this during negotiations as a professional dominatrix. Let me show you what I mean.

One of the most common statements from submissives is, "Whatever makes you happy. Whatever you want to do." I get it. They don't want to be seen to be controlling the scene when, for them, giving up control is the whole point of the interaction. But beyond that, the point is mutual satisfaction, right? And "whatever you want to do" isn't exactly conducive to their pleasure when my response is, "Great! Then you won't mind if I strip you naked, douse you in honey, tie you to a tree, and take all of your money!" [Insert evil laugh here.]

Suddenly, these submissives discover information that they wanted to share with me about their needs, limits, and boundaries. And that communication is a gift to me because it means I don't have to read their minds or just try things in the hope that they'll make a connection when in fact that could end up going very, very wrong.

The moral of the story? Communication is a gift.

That's true outside of the bedroom, too. Saying what we need clearly, directly, with compassion and gratitude, is one of the most generous things we can do in an interaction with another human being.

When we communicate clearly, the other person no longer has to wonder what we want, and we no longer have to wonder whether they understand. See the vicious cycle? The assumption that others can read our minds is often the biggest obstacle to getting what we need—and feeling good about it.

Let's take the everyday, relatively simple example of ordering food from a waiter. In this interaction, I assume the waiter wants to know very clearly what I'm looking for in my meal, and I want to give him all the information I possibly can to allow him to do his job. Say you don't want mayonnaise on your sandwich. It may feel awkward and burdensome to ask whether the sandwich comes with mayonnaise and then request that they keep it off yours. Furthermore, if that sandwich shows up with mayo anyway, it might feel uncomfortable to politely send it back to be redone. But wouldn't it be worse if you ended up with a sandwich you didn't like? You'd be unhappy, you'd feel like you wasted your money and your time, and the waiter would know he sent a customer home frustrated. But by engaging in that moment of clear communication—no matter how awkward it may feel in the moment—you empower the waiter to do his job well, and you ensure you get exactly what you want.

While ordering a meal is a low-pressure situation, the assertiveness we can practice at the table translates into larger experiences. When the stakes *are* high, we're already accustomed to clearly and effectively informing others of our boundaries—and holding others to them if they slip up. After all, how can someone make an informed decision if they're not informed? How can they meet our needs if they don't know them?

Information—communication—is a gift, and when you start looking at it that way, you'll start to perceive your "permission" to communicate your needs in a whole new light. If your boss is constantly interrupting "urgent" tasks with new "urgent" tasks, you're doing them a favor by pausing to give him some information. Remind him—clearly and without emotion—what you're already working on and ask him which project should be prioritized. He may not remember that he'd asked you to tackle that first project, or it may no longer be as urgent as he'd originally thought, or maybe it is, and you ask for another team member to help triage. But you'll burn out if you bite your tongue and juggle everything on your own, and your boss will be left with half-finished work or missed deadlines. When you communicate your needs clearly, you and the other person are both enabled to achieve the results you want.

As I've gotten older, I've gotten better at assuming positive intent—that people are not trying to screw me over or wear me down or take advantage of me. So when their requests or their behavior signal otherwise, rather than fly off the handle or huff off, I try to communicate clearly to ensure that I understand the intent behind the other person's request, that the other person understands the implications of what they're asking, and that I have everything I need to make us both successful.

For example, when someone asks us women what's wrong, we're infamous for angrily saying, "Nothing's wrong!" This comes from our ingrained belief that a) expressing our needs is burdensome and b) others can and should read our minds. But let's assume the person who asks what's wrong really wants to know—and really wants to help, if possible. **By clearly, calmly, and respectfully explaining what's wrong, we give the other person the tools to help us work through the problem, and we give ourselves the gift of building a stronger connection with another person.**

I'll say it again. Communication is a gift, not a burden. When you communicate your needs, you're giving a gift, because you're not expecting them to read your mind and you're taking responsibility for your part in the conversation. If you look at interrupting—or contradicting or even clarifying—as being rude or as indicating that you don't care what others think, then of course you're going to have a hard time setting boundaries and expressing your needs. But if you consider these actions to indicate you're an active participant in the conversation and that you're working toward a common goal, that will shift what it means for you to speak up. The first step to setting boundaries is a huge internal shift in the way you perceive your own communication.

GO DEEPER: REFLECT ON MISCOMMUNICATIONS

- Think about a recent disagreement you had with a friend, colleague, or partner, or a time when your needs weren't met. Could you have communicated more clearly in that situation? How might it have gone if you had?

Saying No

I love the word no. No is a complete sentence. No, I don't need you to rephrase it, and I don't need to qualify it. I said exactly what I meant.

And yet, "no" is one of the hardest boundaries to set. We've been conditioned to take care of others, so saying "no" to a request often feels like doing something wrong.

In reality, setting boundaries around your time and attention is super healthy, and sometimes abundance and connection grows out of saying no rather than yes. Think of it this way: when you say no to spending money, your bank account grows. Or if you say no to an event you really don't want to attend, that means you have more solo time or time with your loved ones.

TAKE ACTION: JUST SAY NO

If you're someone who struggles to say no, then it's time to push outside of your comfort zone and *give no a go*. For the next week, whenever someone asks you to do something you really don't want to do, say no without any further explanation. Fight the urge to soften the no and simply say, "Thank you, but no."

CHAPTER 16

Eliminating Soft Language

BEING A DOMINATRIX GAVE ME an incredible opportunity to practice the clear communication we've been talking about. It was my job to use decisive language and to turn everything into a command. With my clients, it wouldn't be appropriate to request or ask for things. There needed to be an element of demand in every interaction.

But that doesn't mean that I was rude or loud or acted like a jerk. One of my common sayings in kink and life is, "Being an asshole doesn't make you dominant; it just makes you an asshole."

Instead, I had to imbue everything I said with a confident authority and an expectation that they wanted nothing more than to fulfill my every requirement.

It turns out that this has been a useful tool in everyday life too.

One of the most common ways the Bitch Stigma affects women is in the way we communicate. Because women are often socialized to be nice and polite, we lean on "soft language" to pad our messages and protect our audiences. But it often backfires and makes us sound unconfident and in need of reassurance.

Soft language includes things like apologizing—"Oh, I'm sorry but I just wanted to talk to you about..."—and using diminishing or minimizing phrases like, "I was just thinking..." or "Maybe we could consider..."

Before you know it, a simple request turns into, "I was thinking that maybe if you wouldn't mind talking about some ideas that I had, of course we don't have to do them, but..."

Our sentences become three times longer because we're padding them with softening language. What's worse, it's no longer clear what we're even saying or why anyone should care. But, of course, if we just get to the point, we fear we'll come off as curt, bitchy, or nagging.

Here are some examples of softening language:

- Apologizing all the time

- Being sorry for simply "taking up space"

- Qualifying statements with "maybe," "should we consider," or "if you think we should"

- Starting all sentences with "I feel" or "I think" or "I believe"

- Starting sentences with "Can I just say something..."

- Downplaying your own knowledge with "Maybe I'm wrong, but..."

- Saying "just" a lot (I was just thinking, etc.)

- Using a lot of exclamation points, speaking in a really perky way, or making everything you say sound like a question

- Frequently allowing people to talk over you

- Ending sentences with "Don't you agree?" or "What do you think?" or "If it's okay with you…"

This kind of language is sneaky too. Now that I've been retired as a dominatrix for quite a few years I find it creeping back in if I don't watch myself.

Now let's take a look at one of the biggest ones in more depth.

Sorry, Not Sorry: Stop Apologizing

In an effort to appear polite and submissive and avoid the "bitch" category, women say, "I'm sorry," for practically everything. We apologize for taking up space. If somebody else bumps into us in the store, we apologize because we were in their way (even if we weren't actually in their way). Even if a situation simply *feels* awkward—because there's a gap in conversation or for any other minute reason—we apologize.

Sometimes I end up coming off as more of a bitch than I mean to simply because I am conscientiously avoiding some of the expected feminine communication techniques.

For example, I am by no means a professional photographer, but I do have a pretty decent camera, and I recently volunteered my time to take photos at a board meeting for an organization I belong to. After the event I was looking through all the photos, and I noticed that one of the camera settings appeared to be off. There was a slight orange tint. I felt very conflicted when send-ing the photos out to the board about whether I should apologize.

My instinct was to say, "I'm so sorry that these are not per-fect. That the lighting is not better. That I'm not as familiar with the camera as I'd like to be." But of course, if I hadn't been there, we wouldn't have had any photos at all. As a result, an internal conflict was created. Do I apologize and downgrade my contribution, or do I skip it to avoid bolstering the assumption that women should apologize for every little inconvenience, whether it merits an apology or not? (Ultimately, I decided not to apologize but to file this away as a reminder to be more aware of camera settings and deliver better photos in the future.)

When we apologize all the time it appears that we're taking responsibility for other people or for inconsequential or accidental occurrences. That's because we are. That's because we have been taught to do so.

We also use the phrase "I'm sorry" to express empathy rather than as an actual apology. It's a way of acknowledging what someone else is going through when you don't know what else to say. While this instance isn't as much about apologizing as about expressing solidarity, it still reinforces the tendency to say "I'm sorry" in situations that don't call for it.

In short, there's almost always a better option than "I'm sorry." Here are some suggestions:

- Offer a solution: Rather than focusing on a mistake that was made, skip straight to correcting it. "I didn't include this information in the last email. You can find additional details below."

- Shift from regret to gratitude: Instead of "I'm so sorry this is late!" say, "Thank you for your patience."

- Focus on solidarity, if that's what you mean: Rather than, "I'm sorry you're going through that," say, "That sounds so frustrating. I'm not sure how to help, but I'm here for you."

Other phrases that can come in handy when avoiding excessive apologizing:

- Good catch, I'll make the updates/changes.

- Thanks for bringing this to my attention.

- Excuse me, pardon me, or go ahead.

- Could you clarify...

- I have a question about...

- Thank you for the invitation, but I'm not able to make it.

- I appreciate the input, but we need to move onto the next point.

"Sorry" is a reflex, but there are lots of other things you can say instead, and often you don't need to say anything at all. If you really have done something to ruffle someone's feathers, but you haven't done anything wrong, "I regret..." is a much better alternative. When I make a decision and it impacts somebody else negatively, but I've made the decision that I need to make, I can say, "I regret that you are having this experience," without actually apologizing for taking care of my own needs. That's a big one.

MINIMIZING DIMINISHING LANGUAGE

While it's fine to be polite and consider how your communication will be received, there's a balance, and too much soft language will only diminish what you have to say.

Soft language should be a choice, not a default. There are times when softening your language is appropriate, such as when being apologetic or being overly solicitous about something is a benefit or an authentic act. Maybe you're starting a relationship, or maybe the other person needs that in order to successfully receive what you're trying to say. I'm all for using these things as tools when necessary, but not feeling trapped by them.

GO DEEPER: IDENTIFYING YOUR SOFT LANGUAGE HABITS

- What kind of soft language do you use most frequently?

- How does it feel to imagine not using those soft language techniques anymore?

- Where do you need to start with removing soft language? In your emails? At work? Where else?

TAKE ACTION: WRITE STRONGER EMAILS

Removing soft language from written communication has been one of the most powerful things I've done. I write something out and then I go back and remove every single apologetic-sounding phrase. I usually also have to remove a few exclamation points that I've included because I think they'll make me sound happier. Really, all they do is diminish my authority.

Goals: Stop using questions to make statements. Be declarative. Use short sentences. Don't rely on excessive perkiness.

Step one: Go back through the emails you've written in the last week or two. Identify places where you explicitly apologize, where you soften your language, and where you otherwise "kneecap" your writing. Make a note of what your patterns are and what you need to especially keep an eye out for as you practice communicating with more strength.

Step two: Now it's time to start changing your habits. This week, reread every email before you hit send and remove these words:

- I'm sorry

- Sort of

- Kind of

- Maybe

- I hope that

- Or whatever

- Just

- Can you (especially when you're the boss)

- I think, or in my opinion

There's even a Google Chrome/Gmail plug-in to help with this. "Just Not Sorry" warns you when you write emails using words that undermine your message.49

TAKE ACTION: TAKE A SORRY DETOX

While you're working on removing soft language from your writing, practice removing it from your speech too. Focus on one word or phrase per week and remove them from your vocabulary one at a time.

It's a "Sorry Detox." You can even put a dollar in a jar every time you accidentally say it, then treat yourself with something fabulous once you've broken the habit. (If putting money in a jar isn't an effective or feasible reward system for you, you can personalize it to anything that will motivate you to track your behavior.)

Print out a copy of the grid below (you can find it at Bitch-Stigma.com/Library) to post next to your computer so you're ready with some options other than sorry.

TAKE ACTION: SPEAK WITH STRENGTH

Start speaking with clearer authority. Think of it as making micro-assertions. Make statements instead of asking questions. You can still be polite without speaking in a way that is overly apologetic or diminishing to yourself.

INSTEAD OF THIS:	TRY THIS:	
"Oh, I'm so sorry, I can't believe I messed that up!"	"Good catch! Thanks for bringing it to my attention."	"I'm glad you spotted that. I'll make the change."
"Can I just say something?"	"Here's what I think..."	[Or just saying it!]
[Allowing someone whose opinion you don't need to speak over you]	"Thanks for the input, but we need to move on to the next point."	"Your opinion has been noted."
"Oh, I'm so sorry you're experiencing that."	"That sounds frustrating. I'm not sure how to help, but I'm here for you."	"Let me know how I can support you."

INSTEAD OF THIS:	TRY THIS:	
"I'm sorry, I'm trying to get past."	"Can I get past really quick? Thanks!"	"Excuse me."
"Oh no, I'm so sorry but I can't do [insert anything here]."	"Thanks for the invitation, but I can't make it."	"I can't take that on right now, but thanks for thinking of me."
"I'm sorry, I don't understand."	"Could you clarify…"	"Let me see if I understand."
"I'm sorry I wasn't clear."	"Thanks for asking clarifying questions, here's additional information…"	"Let me put it another way."
"I'm sorry, I need you to…"	"I need you to…thanks!"	"Would it work for you to…?"
"Oh, I'm so sorry I'm running late, [insert lengthy excuse here]."	"Thank you for patience…"	"I appreciate you waiting for me."

CHAPTER 17

Dealing with Mansplainers & Conversational Bulldozers

ANOTHER SOFTENING TECHNIQUE IS ALLOWING other people to speak over us. Our language becomes so soft that we just stop talking, and we allow people to talk and talk and talk. Sometimes the person doing the talking is a mansplainer and sometimes they're a conversational bulldozer. What's the difference? Gender and power.

Let's talk about the difference between mansplaining and conversational bulldozing. Here's how I define the terms:

Mansplaining is a very specific style of communication. It's not simply any time a man opens his mouth. Mansplaining occurs when a man speaks condescendingly to a woman under the (often incorrect) assumption that he knows more about the subject than she does simply because he's a man. Mansplaining is specifically rooted in the power dynamics of gender.

The term is commonly credited to Rebecca Solnit, who used it in her 2008 essay "Men Explain Things to Me," which became a book in 2014.[50]

The term "mansplaining" is pointing out an inequitable power differential that allows men to feel entitled to women's attention and dismiss their expertise. It's punching up. Other terms like "womansplaining" are punching down. They may refer to the same action, but when a woman "'splains" something, she's not doing it from the same place of social power as a man. In order to put mansplaining and womansplaining on the same plane really reinforces—rather than reduces—the inequitable power differential.

Conversational bulldozing, on the other hand, is a much less intentional form of interruption that occurs when one person dominates a conversation without truly realizing what he or she is doing. Conversational bulldozers can be people of any gender. Sometimes it's motivated by obliviousness, as some people just really don't realize how much they're talking. Sometimes it's motivated by a power dynamic, as when someone consciously or unconsciously believes that the person talking is the one with the power, so they won't let anyone else get a word in edgewise. Conversational bulldozers interrupt and dominate any discussion they're a part of.

What they both have in common is disrespect (intentional or not) for the person they're in conversation with.

I separate the difference between mansplaining and conversational bulldozing by looking at intention (conscious or not) and any power dynamic involved. Mansplaining is a very specific term that refers to a very specific dynamic. When men are mansplaining, they're often trying to establish and assert their authority, their expertise, and their place in the hierarchy.

"Boys are expected to play by different rules, since the social organization of boys is different. Boys' groups tend to be more obviously hierarchical: Someone is one-up, and someone is one-down. Boys don't typically accuse each other of being "bossy" because the high-status boys are expected to give orders and push the low-status boys around."

—DEBORAH TANNEN[51]

There's an implicit bias amongst men that says, "I'm male; therefore, I must know more. Therefore, what I have to say is more important."

Can Men Mansplain to Other Men? Are Men the Only Ones to Take Over Conversations?

The answer is no, and no. When men mansplain it creates an inherently different social experience than when women or non-male-identified folks simply bulldoze a conversation. This is why I also use the phrase "conversational bulldozer" because there are times when sexism *isn't* at play (though toxic masculinity can certainly be a factor when men talk to men), and goodness knows it's not just men who won't shut up sometimes.

I can be a conversational bulldozer myself, because I don't wait for people to ask me what I think. I take responsibility for my own communication and I tell them what I think. But here's the thing. That's not how other people experience it. Other people experience it as me talking over them or me not caring about what they have to say. I care deeply about what (some) other people have to say, but my natural communication style can prevent those conversations from feeling successful. It took me decades to really recognize that. Also, while men over-explain to other men all the time, the difference is that there isn't a social power dynamic inherent to the interaction, and the options men have for stopping that kind of conversation are a lot more varied (and likely more well-received) than when women try to stop men from over-explaining (and are then more likely to be labeled a bitch).

"When a man gives his opinion, he's a man. When a woman gives her opinion, she's a bitch."

—BETTE DAVIS, ACTRESS

Another example of conversation hijacking is the even newer term "manteruption" to describe the common imbalance of how much men and women talk in a conversation. A study from Brigham Young University and Princeton discovered that during board meetings, men dominate 75 percent of the conversation. Another study by empirical linguist Kieran Snyder found that "men interrupt at twice the rate of women and are three times more likely to interrupt women as to interrupt other men."[52]

Deborah Tannen, a linguistics expert, has a series of books on communication that are an in-depth explanation of gendered communication.

"Both claims—that men interrupt women and that women interrupt men—reflect and bolster the assumption that an interruption is a hostile act, a kind of conversational bullying. The interrupter is seen as a malevolent aggressor, the interrupted an innocent victim."

—DEBORAH TANNEN, YOU JUST DON'T UNDERSTAND: WOMEN AND MEN IN CONVERSATION[53]

But it's not always that way. I should note here that mansplaining isn't always about pushing women down. I feel a lot of compassion for men because they are trapped in their own gendered expectations. The flip side of the Bitch Stigma is what I call the Macho Mindset, which is in line with toxic masculinity and men's socially ingrained need to be the highest authority in the room. That's often tied very deeply to their own identity and sense of self-worth.

Sometimes mansplaining is intentionally malicious and condescending, and sometimes it really is just oblivious. This section isn't about bashing men. It's about providing women a tool to deal with a particular situation.

Identifying Mansplainers Versus Bulldozers

One of the ways that mansplainers and conversational bulldozers get room to do what they do is because of women's inherent tendency to soften our language and be polite at all costs. No matter how rude somebody else is being, we don't want to sink to their level. We just stand there and let them talk because we think we're doing the polite thing. That also backfires.

The right moment and way to deal with someone talking over you is different depending on the situation. Sometimes it's appropriate to call it out in the moment, even if it happens to be in front of people. But sometimes it's more appropriate to find a private moment to say something like, "Hey, can I talk to you for a second? I think we missed the mark on this conversation, and I want to establish a better understanding going forward."

But either way, it's important to address the situation before it becomes a pattern. Of course, that's often easier said than done, and part of the difficulty is that calling out other people is uncomfortable for both parties, so we've spent our lives avoiding it. Because of that, we don't have a sense memory that helps us know how to call things out in the moment. That's why so many of us have experienced the frustration of realizing exactly what we should have said an hour or more later.

I was invited to speak to a small group for a sextech meetup, and the experience gave me great examples for identifying the difference between mansplaining and bulldozing and handling them accordingly.

I was one of two speakers, and while the other was telling her story, two women entrepreneurs started talking over her because they were so excited about their business and wanted to share how it related. I loved their excitement, but I didn't love that they kept interrupting and talking over the invited speaker. So I waited for them to take a breath, and I said, "It's so fascinating to hear about your journey, and I'd love to hear more about your business during the networking portion, and to turn it back to you [the other speaker] I'd really love to hear you elaborate on [this topic]." Then I turned and looked expectantly at my fellow speaker. For the women in the audience, it was enthusiasm and not ego that was pushing them to overtake the conversation, so I pivoted politely back to the speaker in a way that wouldn't make the attendees feel scolded or embarrassed.

When it was my turn to talk, I was commenting about how the adult industry does tend to attract non-traditional folks, many of whom have good intentions but are unreliable. I was saying that in the adult industry, you have to be careful who you work with, because not everyone is as interested in the realistic hard work as they are in the mythical glamour. At that point, a man in the group said, "I think what Kali is trying to say is that there are bad people in every industry, and you have to watch out." Now, when I look at my Mirror Matrix on my very best, most badass day, I am 100 percent Rogue. So I looked at the man and responded accordingly: "That's actually not at all what I said. That's what *you* said. I'm going to come back to what I said. I'm going to reiterate it because we're talking about my experience right now."

The difference in the two interrupters—and in my responses to each—was distinct. You want to encourage enthusiasm like the women bulldozers within the bounds of what's respectful to the people around you. But this man's interjection wasn't based on enthusiasm. He was trying to assert his knowledge, his opinion, and his expertise by undermining mine. So, I took a more firm, direct approach to let him know I wasn't interested in playing his game.

Now, if you're not sure whether the person talking over you is a mansplainer or just a bulldozer, try to figure out their motivation. Is it enthusiasm? Is it arrogance? Is it refusal to see your expertise? Is it because they have a different conversational style? All of those things impact how you respond.

In this mansplainer's case, I shut that shit down. I wasn't rude, but I wasn't going to let him talk over me or change my message to suit him.

You're Not Talking Too Much

Before we move on to tactics that will help you shut down mansplainers and change the dynamic with bulldozers, let me say one very important thing: If you're being mansplained or bulldozed, it is not because you are talking too much. You don't deserve to be talked over simply because you've said more words than some arbitrary rule deems appropriate.

The myth that women talk more than men has been completely debunked at this point, but it's one of those "old wives' tales" that persists. That very phrase feeds the myth! In fact, in most groups that researchers from Brigham Young University and Princeton studied, the time women spoke was significantly less than their proportional representation—amounting to less than 75 percent of the time men spoke.[54]

Want to see for yourself? Here's another fun little resource called Are Men Talking Too Much, a simple online counter that allows you to compare how often "a dude" versus "not a dude" are talking in a meeting or conversation.[55]

It's long past time to ditch any concerns that you have that you're talking more than other people, because that's not likely happening.

Got it? Good. Now let's move on.

How to Stop a Mansplainer or Conversational Bulldozer

People don't perceive themselves as rude. And most people aren't self-aware enough to think, "She really changed her energy there. I wonder what I might have said." That kind of reflection just isn't a real priority in our current culture.

So how do we get it through their heads?

Body language alone won't make an impact on the bulldozer—we have to call them out verbally.

To become comfortable doing that, we have to exercise the muscle and get used to potentially being considered rude. I don't like to be rude. I was raised to be a nice person. I am a nice person. But here's the way that I shifted my mentality: I will not hesitate to match actual rudeness with (potentially perceived) rudeness. If somebody is talking over me and won't let me get a word in edgewise, they're already being rude. That's them. I'm not going to match it with asshole behavior, but I'm going to let them take responsibility for how they're behaving. I'll say, "I'm going to have you stop right there. I'm already familiar with what you're talking about, but I'd love to hear you talk about this other thing that I don't know about."

Everyone has their own authentic way of speaking up that feels natural to them. I use humor a lot (though it can sometimes miss the mark if the other person doesn't have a sense of humor). I might say, "You're just really committed to finishing that sentence, huh? You're in it till the end." And then I look at them with a smile. Or I might say, "I actually don't need a human encyclopedia right now, but I appreciate you volunteering for the job!" If they don't take it as a compliment, they get the message that it's time for them to shut up and let me talk.

Humor works for me, but it is not going to work for a lot of people, so we'll cover several strategies based on each of our Bold Badass archetypes. You'll find one that works for you.

But whatever your style, there is one universal rule:

Speak up *before* you're pissed off! Speak up sooner! If you wait until you're ready to explode, then of course your emotions and your anger are going to come out and undermine your boldness and expertise. Speak up before your patience runs out, and practice shutting down the interruptions earlier and earlier. Even if this time it's just three minutes earlier than last time, then five minutes earlier, you're making progress. The moment that you start to feel yourself thinking, "I don't need to know this. I don't need to listen to you," that's when you need to say something.

I always start with a pleasant, fun tone because I assume they just don't realize what they're doing. Like I said before, assume positive intent. It'll keep you sane. Lower the stakes for yourself—the interrupters are either in this conversation with you or they're not, and if they don't want to hear about your experiences or your perspective, is this a conversation you need to value? Remembering these two theories will help you muster the confidence to speak up before you get to the point where you want to metaphorically (or actually) punch your interrupter in the face. Calmly, lightly, say something like, "Thanks for the info, but I have it covered," or, "We don't need to go any deeper into that subject, but thanks!"

There is a chance that your assertion is going to make the other person feel like they're not being listened to, but I don't care. We're so concerned with everyone else feeling heard that we deny our own opportunity to be heard.

Sometimes, in an effort to maintain power or avoid embarrassment, the interruptor will turn it back around and start grilling you with questions. It's a common response to blush and stammer and end up feeling like you look worse. When this happens, the interruptor is trying to make you feel like you have to prove yourself in order to gain their respect. That's another game I refuse to play. Wherever you are, you deserve to be there as much as the next person, and you have the right to ensure your voice is heard without having to defend yourself.

THE POWER OF INTERRUPTION

When the bulldozers and mansplainers get going, our socially ingrained hesitance to interrupt gets in our way. I get it, we don't want to be rude, and interrupting feels rude. But when it comes to managing people who talk over us, we have to get over that right now.

Here's why: The longer the mansplainer talks, the smaller we become in their eyes. They're "teaching us all these things" and positioning us as the student who needs to learn. We all know that's a load of crap.

But since interrupting is an uncomfortable notion, let's reframe it to make it more palatable for the purposes of this conversation. Let's call it "strategic interrupting."

If the bulldozer or mansplainer won't stop talking, you officially have my permission to interrupt them. You're not being rude; you're not talking over someone. You're simply insisting on the right to finish your thought.

But once you've decided you're ready to interrupt the interrupter, what are you going to say? When you're first starting to implement this tool, coming up with the right line can be difficult. Again, you don't have the muscle memory because you haven't done this before.

I'm going to give you some suggested phrases throughout the rest of this chapter. I recommend that you practice them. It's the only way to build that muscle and to build that sense memory so that when you're in a high energy, high anxiety, high pressure situation, you'll already know what to do. You might feel silly practicing these strategic interruptions in the car or in the shower, but I guarantee that it will help. (As always, it's even better to practice with a person.)

More often than not, "I wasn't actually quite finished," is a good place to start. If somebody interrupts me to start mansplaining or bulldozing, I'll say "Let me finish this thought, and then I'd love to hear what you have to say." A lot of times people just need to know that there will be space for them to be heard.

Or you could get into a conversational battle. Just say, "Oh yes I'm already familiar with such and such," and then YOU start explaining, so they've got to be the one to interrupt you.

Whatever you say to interrupt the interrupter—and that will depend on where you fall on the Mirror Matrix—the most important thing to do after that is to just keep talking. It's tough to do, but you can't wait for their approval if you want to take back the floor. Just keep talking, and then when they try to keep talking over you, interrupt them again: "Oop, nope, not quite yet. It'll be your turn in just a minute." Then, again, *keep talking*.

I say it. I try to use body language. I try to use tone. I look them in the eye so that they're still feeling seen. But I've found the most foundational piece is the promise that they'll get their turn to be heard as soon as I'm done. You've got to find the wording that you'll actually feel comfortable saying, because, "I'll give you your turn in a minute," is definitely on the higher end of the bitch spectrum. The exact words aren't necessarily critical, as long as what you're communicating is, "You will get to talk, just not yet."

NOW, WHAT ABOUT DEALING WITH A CHRONIC— BUT INNOCENT—BULLDOZER LIKE ME?

I know I can be exhausting, and I also know that every one of us has a friend like me who just gets so excited to share her thoughts that she runs right over whoever she's talking to. In these situations, there aren't power dynamics at play, or really much ego either. When it comes to getting a little air time back from a friendly bulldozer, your approach can be friendly too.

The kink world uses the term "safe word," and the concept has become much more mainstream lately. A safe word—or a safe gesture—is meant to mean "please stop what you're doing."

My friends and I have come up with a safe gesture for when my bulldozing gets out of control. I've taught my friends to make the shushing motion (with their finger to their lips) when I'm talking too much. When they shush me, I know that they're not trying to say, "Oh my God, why are you still talking. I don't care about what you're saying. Just shut up already." They're saying, "I'm not done yet. Please let me finish talking."

Another time, I was slipping into Fanatic mode in a conversation, and a friend had the perfect response. As I was getting more and more intense, she said, "I feel like I have already agreed with you, but I haven't had the chance to share my own opinion. One of the things that I appreciate about you is that you are so definitive in your opinion, but I also want to be able to share my opinion and feel like that opinion is being respected."

Her interjection brought me up short in the best possible way. I didn't feel judged or chastised; instead, I felt like she was communicating directly, compassionately, and with strength, helping me become more aware of myself as she stood her ground at the same time. It made me appreciate having a friend like her.

Whether you're dealing with ego or excitement, when all the subtlety and grace in the world fails you, try naming the behavior outright by saying, "You keep interrupting me. Please let me finish." After all, sometimes you have to hit people over the head to make your point.

Here are some specific things to keep in mind when you need to stop a mansplainer or conversational bulldozer:

- Silent protest and body language will rarely work alone

- If you're with other women, help amplify what they're saying

- I often use humor and a light-hearted approach with increasing firmness if they aren't receptive to the softer redirection

Here's another real-life example: Recently, a man attempted to mansplain to me what being a former dominatrix is like. He's never been a dominatrix. I'm the only dominatrix that he's ever known in his entire life. So, my response to him was, "Well, after eighteen years of being connected to the industry I'm very comfortable with my level of knowledge. If you ever want to learn about my experience, I'd love to sit down with you another time." Then—*Boom!* —I started talking about something else. Because the moment you get into a pissing match, you're right back on the bottom end of the power dynamic. You're allowing them to define you and the conversation.

I've even been known to say, "Oh, I don't need to prove anything, so let's just move the conversation forward." I recognize that kind of cheekiness is part of my personality, but that's why it's important to figure out a phrase you can comfortably and naturally use to regain control of the conversation. Look at these examples and then find wording that is suitable for YOU to express yourself.

"Oh yes! I'm already familiar with _____ so we can move on."

"Thanks for the info, but I have it covered!"

"Thanks, but we don't need to go any deeper into that subject."

"I appreciate you telling me about this. However, what I'm talking about is this right here."

"I'm going to finish this thought, and then I'd love to hear what you think."

"I'd really love to hear your thoughts but just give me a minute. I want to complete this thought of mine to share with you."

"I'd love to hear what you have to say, but let me finish the story and then we'll get right back to you."

You'll notice these phrases include that promise that "your turn is coming" or, at the very least, an acknowledgment that you've heard what they said. If that's still not enough for them, that's when I stop caring, because now we're back to taking responsibility for how other people might potentially feel. Then I pull out the more assertive phrases:

"I'm gonna stop you right there."

"Hey, let me stop you there."

There are times when we need to care, and there are times when it's okay to allow somebody else to think that we're being rude. It's okay to value our own voices, and it's okay to protect our right to be heard, and if we do that firmly but respectfully and our mansplainers or bulldozers are still upset about it, that's on them.

Another helpful option is to put a "no interruption" rule in effect at work or with your loved ones, especially when you're talking about something that's important to you. For example, if you are struggling to implement strategic interruption then before starting a conversation you can preface it with something like, "It's important that I'm able to finish this thought without interruption. I look forward to hearing your thoughts, but please let me finish first."

Archetypes in Action

Scenario: You're at a work meeting sharing a new strategy that you know will benefit your team. A colleague has interrupted you many times in the past and tends to talk over you when you're making a point.

Below are examples of ways women who identify with each of our archetypes *might* handle the situation. Remember, though, that these are just examples that are meant to get you started. You're welcome to take strategies from any archetype or develop your own—just be sure your strategic interruption style feels natural to you.

ADVOCATE:

When they take a breath or pause for even a brief moment say, "Thank you," and start right where you left off when you were interrupted.

WARRIOR:

Interrupt them and say, "I appreciate your enthusiasm but I'm going to finish my thoughts before we move on."

QUEEN:

Make eye contact and say evenly, "I believe it's still my turn. Please let me speak before you share your thoughts."

BOSS:

Hold your hand up in the stop motion and say, "Just a moment. Before you jump in, I'm going to finish this thought."

REBEL:

Lean forward with strong eye contact and say, "I'm being cut short here. Please let me complete my thought, thanks."

ROGUE:

Interrupt them and say, **"I wasn't done talking,"** and just keep right on making the point you were making.

TAKE ACTION: PRACTICE STRATEGIC INTERRUPTING WITH YOUR MUTUAL ADMIRATION SOCIETY

These phrases are particularly important to practice, so it's time to get out there with your MAS (Mutual Admiration Society) or in lower pressure, real life situations (for example, with a friend rather than a work colleague).

If you're practicing with your MAS, swap back and forth so you each have a turn as the conversational bulldozer and as the one speaking up. Try out the different phrases mentioned in this chapter. Come up with your own and write them down.

I'd even recommend putting them on flashcards (either with old-fashioned index cards or an app on your phone) so that you can read through them on a regular basis. The more comfortable and automatic these phrases are for you, the more easily you'll be able to use them when you need them.

CHAPTER 18

Setting Physical Boundaries

AS A DOMINATRIX, I LEARNED how to use my body to communicate boundaries, confidence, and the fact that I am worthy of space.

Setting physical boundaries, such as how close people stand to us or if and how they are allowed to touch us, is another area that's rife with potential to get us labeled a bitch. In situations where we're being touched inappropriately or feeling crowded by someone coming into our space, it's a socialized response for politeness to kick in so we prioritize someone else's needs over our own. But we've already decided that we're not going to do that anymore, so let's look at some new ways we can set physical boundaries while still being respectful to those around us.

When Someone Is in Your Space

When it comes to setting physical boundaries, I like to use direct communication. If somebody is invading my space, then I say in a very friendly but firm tone, "Excuse me. I'm feeling a little bit crowded. Can you back up just a little bit? I appreciate it." Pairing that request with eye contact can be a powerful way of establishing that, even though I'm being friendly, I'm comfortable and in control, and I mean what I said.

Usually, that's all it takes, but occasionally, it's not so easy.

There was one situation where I was at the pharmacy, and there was a man crowding me. I didn't really want him hearing about my private health issues, so I said, "Excuse me, you're getting a little close there. Can you please back up a little bit?" And he said "No." There was plenty of room, but he refused to back off. I made sure that I was standing steady, with my weight distributed evenly so I was facing him squarely and sturdily. I replied, "I'm asking you to respect my reasonable boundaries, and you're refusing to do that. Is that what you're saying?"

Rather than get defensive, I simply articulated the social faux pas *he* was making. And sure enough, he "suddenly remembered" he had to look for something on another shelf. He didn't apologize, but he did back down. The key for me here was that I wasn't disrespecting him but highlighting his disrespect for me.

Get Big

When it comes to protecting ourselves, our instinct is often to take up less space—to shrink away and disappear in the hopes of avoiding or escaping the situation. But in many scenarios, a better bet is to get big, taking up as much space as possible to show others that you're not scared and, furthermore, you'll be a huge pain in the ass if they mess with you.

One day I was walking in my neighborhood not too long after I moved to Boston. The neighborhood was kind of sketchy, so I always walked with purpose and with my head up. On this day, I had picked up some of my favorite food from a local restaurant, and I was on the phone as I walked back to my house.

As I made my way down the side street, I saw three men sitting on a stoop. They'd obviously been drinking. As I walked past, one of them said, "Hey baby, can I get your number?"

This is pretty typical street harassment, so my standard response is to smile and say, "Nope, but have a great day!" and keep walking. Since I was on my phone this time, I just shook my head and kept talking.

Then all three of them got up and started following me.

"Hey baby, he just wants your number. Stop and talk to us for a minute. Hey baby, you're so sexy. We just want to say, hi."

Finally, I stopped talking to my friend on the phone and spoke directly to them. "No thanks, guys. I'm not interested."

That's when their tone changed. They started circling around me, preventing me from moving forward.

"Why do you have to be such a bitch? He just wants to get your number. He just wants to say hi because you're so sexy. Don't be a bitch. Why you gotta be a bitch?"

The interaction went from annoying to unsafe really quickly. I had already changed directions to walk back toward the main street rather than my apartment so they wouldn't know where I lived. I looked around for backup. There was a man in a suit watching this whole thing, but he didn't say a word.

I changed my tone, too. I started moving my arms wildly around me and shouting. "You want to see what a bitch looks like?! You don't know who the FUCK you're dealing with!!"

I walked directly at them, swinging my bag and shouting. Immediately the man in the suit took off, solidifying my suspicion that he was obviously not going to get involved or help in any way. I continued shouting.

"I'm calling the fucking police unless you back the fuck off and leave me the fuck alone. I'll show you what a fucking bitch looks like!"

The three men quickly took off when they realized that I was going to be a lot more trouble than I was worth.

In a world that's constantly trying to make women smaller, there is a value in responding by getting bigger instead. If getting small isn't working for you—especially when your safety is in question and running isn't an option—it's time to get big.

Take Up Space

And being big isn't only about getting out of dangerous situations. Have you ever noticed yourself scrambling to be as small as possible? When we're on public transportation or navigating a crowd, many women tend to shrink ourselves. It's the opposite of man spreading. It's woman shrinking.

We deserve to be on the train or on the sidewalk or wherever we are just as much as any man. For this reason, take up space. If you notice that you scramble to get out of everybody's way on the sidewalk, practice being a little bit slower to move. Of course, this doesn't mean being rude and arrogant—you still need to step aside for seniors and parents with strollers. But if there is an able-bodied man or a group of people walking toward you, try your best to keep your head up, keep walking straight, and let *them* move out of *your* way.

The next time there's a clusterfuck at a door or elevator and everybody's playing the "Oh, no, you first" game, take the lead. Same thing at a four-way stop sign. When nobody is moving, take the lead, and blaze the trail.

"I like being present in spaces where I am not welcome, because you do not deserve to feel comfortable just because you're racist or sexist or small-minded."

—SCAACHI KOUL, WRITER

Another place we can work on taking up space is in crowded restaurants and bars. Say you're the first of your group to arrive, and you snagged four seats at the bar for your friends who are five minutes away. When someone else approaches and asks if the seats are taken, it can be tempting to give them up in order to make space and avoid looking selfish. A simple, direct, "yes" is all you need to say.

On the sidewalk, in a bar, in a coffee shop, or anywhere else you happen to be, you deserve to be there. You don't have to be rude, but you don't have to apologize for taking up space, either.

Hugging and Gray-area Touching

I'm not a hugger. At least not with people I don't know and definitely not with men in a professional capacity. I have a lot of experience dodging and weaving while keeping things light-hearted.

Some folks are naturally more touchy-feely than others, and there's a lot of pressure not to reject physical touching when it's supposedly done affectionately. But the bottom line is that if you're uncomfortable, then they need to adapt to you, not the other way around.

When the behavior is egregious, it's easier for some women to call it out. "Harmless" unwanted touching may feel tougher to set boundaries around, but if it's touching we don't want, then it isn't harmless, no matter what anyone else says. This may seem to be one of those situations where you have to choose your discomfort. Either you let them hug you and are then uncomfortable because another person is touching you, or you don't let them hug you and are uncomfortable because you've risked hurting another person's feelings simply by asserting your own boundaries. However, the discomfort of letting someone touch you when you don't want them to is one you'll feel over and over, every time you receive an unwanted hug.

So instead of thinking of that incoming hug as a lose-lose situation, reframe the encounter as an opportunity to assert your personal boundaries and flex your "no thank you" muscles. The goal is to set your boundaries firmly and naturally, so you don't have to be uncomfortable, and neither does the other person, and that will get easier with practice. But in the end, if standing up for your space means being a bitch, then this is a great opportunity to embrace your inner bitch and ditch the Bitch Stigma.

Archetypes in Action

Scenario: You're at a conference, and a man you are being introduced to makes an obvious move to come in for an intimate hug. His arms are wide open, and he's moving his body towards you, what do you decide to do?

These are a few suggestions, inspired by each archetype, for how to rebuff that hug. Still, remember that it's up to you to find a strategy that feels authentic to your own inner Bold Badass.

ADVOCATE:
Say, "I think I'm getting a cold, I wouldn't want you to catch it," while waving your hands in front of your face and backing up.

WARRIOR:

Extend your hand and say, "I prefer a handshake."

QUEEN:

Stand up straight, maybe even lean back ever so slightly to indicate you're not interested, and say, "It's a pleasure to meet you."

BOSS:

As soon as you see them coming in for a hug, wordlessly extend your hand for a handshake and put a hand on their shoulder or elbow in order to help control the distance between you.

REBEL:

Give them a high five!

ROGUE:

The Duck and Dodge will definitely get the point across. Physically moving around and away from their outstretched arms while saying something like, "I'm not a hugger!" is direct and likely unforgettable.

GO DEEPER: PROTECT YOUR PERSONAL SPACE

- Write about a time your personal space was violated. What would you do differently now?

- Recall a time when you intentionally took up space. How did it feel? (If you can't recall a time, imagine what it might feel like.)

TAKE ACTION: GET BIG

List three ways you're going to practice taking up space in the next week.

You can try one strategy per day, see how it goes, and log your experiences in your journal. Use your gold stars to reward yourself when you push outside of your comfort zone.

Conclusion

"Bitches get stuff done."

—TINA FEY, ACTRESS

SO BE A BITCH. FIERCELY set and enforce your boundaries. You should always be willing to take in new information and come at every situation from a place of positive assumptions and compassion. But other than that, *fuck 'em.* Your boundaries are your boundaries, and nobody else has any right to tell you what those boundaries should be or how you should enforce them. If someone isn't comfortable with you asserting your needs, that's their problem, not yours. When it's a stranger who gets in your way, assert yourself and move on. If it's someone who's a regular in your life, you need to take a look at whether or not that relationship really feeds you and nourishes you, and whether it's something you need in your life. If it's not—if you've been holding onto that relationship out of convenience or kindness or obligation—it may be time to ditch the Bitch Stigma and let go of the relationship.

I look around and see the righteous rage of women, and I think it's a beautiful thing. Women have been waiting for the opportunity to become safer, happier, and more successful, and those things aren't happening fast enough or far enough.

Those things aren't *going* to happen if we keep waiting politely and patiently for them. Right now is an incredibly powerful time, because a lot more women are standing up, and it's always easier to do something when you're not doing it alone.

But remember, confidence is a journey and not a destination. You might take two steps forward and one step back, and that's okay. Be patient with yourself. As you develop and practice new techniques, you'll become more and more comfortable being your authentic, confident self in increasingly difficult conversations. Whatever happens, keep moving forward and giving yourself room to grow.

Don't let fear—fear of rejection, fear of misunderstanding, fear of being labeled a bitch—prevent you from doing exactly what you need to do in your life.

If forcefully designing and curating your life makes you a bitch, then you sew that Scarlet B on your chest, and you wear it with pride.

GO DEEPER: WHERE ARE YOU NOW?

- What has your experience been with reading this book and putting the suggestions into action?

- Is there anything you found especially easy? Is there anything you found especially difficult?

- How did it impact your experience to do it along with your Mutual Admiration Society (if you had one)? If you went through the book alone, what do you think you could get out of it by doing it with friends?

- How are you going to continue to integrate these ideas into your life?

READY TO TAKE ACTION?

I would love to hear which parts of this book resonate with you. Which strategies have changed your life? Which theories made you see things in a new way or say, "Yes!"?— Email yes@bitch-stigma.com to tell me how this book has inspired you to embrace your inner badass and ditch the Bitch Stigma. I'm grateful to all the women who've shared their "Yes!" moments already, and I can't wait to hear yours.

I HOPE YOU LOVED THIS BOOK!

If you did, would you mind leaving a fellow badass
an honest review on Amazon? Thanks so much!
BitchStigma.com/BookReview

BONUS!

Remember, I've created a whole set of fun, printable worksheets and templates at BitchStigma.com/library.

You can head there now if you haven't already and download the worksheets and journal pages that will help you *Go Deeper* and *Take Action* so you can take what you've learned and put it into practice in your life.

CONTRIBUTE TO MY NEXT BOOK

In an effort to share more perspectives than my own, I'm working on a followup to *Ditch the Bitch Stigma*, a book of interviews showing how diverse women have come up with unique coping mechanisms to find success and moderate the impact the Bitch Stigma has on their lives.

If you'd like to share your experiences, please fill out my surveys at BitchStigma.com/surveys

HIRE ME AS A SPEAKER

Are you interested in bringing me into your organization to help your people learn how to use confidence and influence to become more effective and powerful communicators? Find more information at KaliWilliams.com

JOIN ME AT A RETREAT OR IN A COACHING SESSION

Would you like to work with me directly? I offer one-on-one and group coaching programs as well as in-person retreats through-out the year. Find more information at BitchStigma.com

Resources

Find Other Resources to Improve These Skills

Practicing the exercises and tools I've given you in this book will take you a long way, but there are many other outlets to help you to take action and improve your new skills.

MAKING FRIENDS

Along with the suggestions you read in the Mutual Admiration Society building section, you can also check out the Bitch Stigma Meetup group to see if there's a chapter near you. BitchStigma. com/Meetup

IMPROV CLASSES

This is one of my personal favorites. Many community colleges, adult continuing ed organizations, and even some comedy clubs offer a variety of improv classes and experiences.

Improv helps develop a lot of skills, but it primarily helps people get more comfortable thinking on their feet and responding quickly to the situations they're in. Practicing these skills in a fun, supportive atmosphere whose core tenet is "Yes, and…" will help you be ready to respond in less pleasant situations.

VOICE LESSONS

A lot of women have naturally softer speaking voices, and the social and environmental training to be sweet and gentle has led to a lot of vocal fry and uptalk. Whether natural or learned, these speaking patterns tend to make us sound less forceful and confident, but one way to combat these concerns is by taking voice lessons. If you tend to speak quietly, a voice coach can teach you to project by speaking from your diaphragm. You can learn to control the tone and projection of your voice, helping you sound as in command as you feel.

PUBLIC SPEAKING

It's a common saying that more people in the United States fear public speaking than death. But it's a surefire way to get more comfortable speaking up, even when you don't technically have an audience. I recommend taking a public speaking class or joining Toastmasters to get practice speaking confidently in front of others. (As a bonus, if you say "like" or "um" frequently, this can be a particularly helpful way to move past those habits.)

SELF-DEFENSE

If physical boundaries are a challenge for you, try taking a self-defense class. If you're concerned about being safe, learning how to physically defend yourself is an excellent way to build the mental and physical confidence so you'll know what to do in case of an actual attack. IMPACT is a national organization with chapters in most large cities that offer woman-focused and LGBTQ workshops specifically to help these communities gain confidence and concrete skills for self defense.

CYBER DEFENSE

A lot of us spend a lot of time online, and there are challenges to staying safe. The last few years have seen an extra upsurge in online doxxing (publishing private or identifying information about a particular individual on the Internet, typically with malicious intent). It's natural to worry about whether or not you'll be perceived as a bitch online and whether that will have any scary repercussions. There are special ways you can protect your privacy as much as possible. I'd highly recommend *The Smart Girl's Guide to Privacy: Practical Tips for Staying Safe Online* by Violet Blue to go step-by-step through your online profiles to protect yourself.

Acknowledgements

THIS BOOK HAS BEEN MANY, many years in the making. It's exhilarating to hold this book in my hands and know that its completion is just the beginning of a whole new chapter in my life of sharing it with the world. I truly couldn't have brought these ideas out of my mind and conversations and into concrete form without the support of all of these incredible folks.

I want to start with the massive gratitude I feel for Sarah Welch, my developmental editor, as well as Rachel Carter, my copyeditor, and Sara Kocec, owner of Yellowbird Editors. Sarah is a brilliant editor and writing teammate, and she did a phenomenal job of polishing my words while staying true to my voice. She worked with me through the entire process, and this book wouldn't be what it is today without her.

My dear one, words can't express the deep ocean of gratitude I feel for all the tangible ways you have supported me in reaching my dreams of bringing this book into the world. I know that no matter where in the world we each are, that you are rooting me on, and I hope you know that I am doing the same. Love you always.

To Robbie Samuels, my accountability buddy and long-distance high-fiver, goes my deep appreciation for the weekly listening sessions, pep talks, and problem solving. Thank you for all your generosity and for truly inspiring me to invest in my relationships in new and deeper ways.

I'm eternally grateful to my friend, Opn, for all of her amazing brainstorming, soundboarding, and editing on not just this book, but everything I do. I'm lucky to have such a helpful and clever BFF. Thanks for everything!

Thank you to my mastermind, brainstorming, and accountability groups for sharing such discerning ongoing feedback and unending support and encouragement: Zaedryn, Marcia, Janet, Ann, Julie, Mindy, and Iris.

Big thanks to my Meetup groups who are full of women who have been a joy to get to know. Especially these women who took the time to speak with me and share their experiences: Mari, Melina, Christine, Spyce, Jill, and Linette. Also big thanks go to everyone who filled out my surveys and the women I initially interviewed in 2017 when I was first forming this book for wide-ranging and informative conversations. Thank you for sharing your time and experiences: Waukeshia, Eva, Nnena, Susan, Sara, and Nicole.

My deep gratitude goes to the wonderfully supportive people who interviewed me and brainstormed with me to get the content, and to my beta readers for sharing such insightful feedback to help me publish the strongest book possible. This shout-out goes to Megara, Brooke, Miray, Brian, Taylor, Gray, Mindy, Earl, Lisa, Julie, Sharon, Zaedryn, Vivienne, Terry, and my mom.

Thank you to Sarah Mason who's been doing my transcription work for years and who has been a vital part of the process of getting my words onto the page. Thank you to my headshot photographer, Benjy Feen, for doing such a great job capturing the sparkle in my eye.

Thank you to my branding and cover designer, Hannah Portello-Swagel, for all the stylish work done to bring the spirit of *Ditch the Bitch Stigma* to life. Thanks also to the Draft Lab team, Lari Bishop and Alex Head, for doing such a stellar job on the inner page design and formatting.

My forever thanks go to my glorious dominatrix and kink friends I've made and kept throughout the last twenty years. You have shown me the many faces of power, confidence, and general badassery. Thank you for all the unique adventures; the kink world will always be my heart and center.

A very special thanks goes to my friends and family who had to listen to me talk through the content over and over and helped me brainstorm and fine-tune these ideas. Thank you to my Facebook friends for giving me so much encouragement and always rooting me on.

Lastly, I'm going to do the Badass Bitch thing and also acknowledge myself! This book is the result of decades of observing, teaching, learning, and paying attention. This book is the result of a sustained and disciplined effort that stretched me out of my comfort zone and I'm proud of myself. We should never feel ashamed to shout out our accomplishments! You can read about the journey at BitchStigma.com/BookJourney.

Endnotes

Introduction

1   https://www.goodgirlrecovery.com/

2   https://leanin.org/

Chapter 1: What's in a Word

3   Richard Lei, "To B. or Not to B.," *The Washington Post*, January 12, 1995, https://www.washingtonpost.com/archive/lifestyle/1995/01/12/to-b-or-not-to-b/b3b29840-81dc-4c5a-86f9-6435d33527b7/?noredirect=on

4   Eyder Peralta, "Sheryl Sandberg: The Word 'Bossy' Should Be Banned," NPR, March 9, 2014, https://www.npr.org/sections/thetwo-way/2014/03/09/288307452/sheryl-sandberg-the-word-bossy-should-be-banned

5   *Wikipedia*, s.v. "Bitch (Slang)," last modified August 21, 2019, https://en.wikipedia.org/wiki/Bitch_(slang)

6   Meghan Neal, "Take It Back: 5 Steps to Reclaim a Dirty Name," Good, July 19, 2012, https://www.good.is/articles/take-it-back-5-steps-to-reclaim-a-dirty-name

7   Adam D. Galinksy et al., "The Reappropriation of Stigmatizing Labels: The Reciprocal Relationship Between Power and Self-Labeling," *Psychological Science*, August 16, 2013, https://journals.sagepub.com/doi/abs/10.1177/0956797613482943?legid=sppss%3B0956797613482943v1&patientinform-links=yes

8   Atlantic Records (2009). Trina – *Da Baddest Bitch* [Video]. Retrieved March 25, 2019 from https://www.youtube.com/watch?v=ABZDZY5aCLY

9 MeredithBrooksVEVO (2010). *Meredith Brooks – Bitch (Official Video)* [Video]. Retrieved March 25, 2019 from https://www.youtube.com/watch?v=_ivt_N2Zcts

10 https://www.bitchmedia.org/

11 Elizabeth Wurtzel, *Bitch: In Praise of Difficult Women*, (New York, Anchor Books, 1998), 29.

12 *Parks and Recreation.* "Gin It Up!" Season 6, episode 5. Directed by Jorma Taccone. Written by Matt Murray. NBC, October 17, 2013.

13 Gary Nunn, "Power Grab: Reclaiming Words Can Be Such a Bitch," *The Guardian*, October 30, 2015, https://www.theguardian.com/media/mind-your-language/2015/oct/30/power-grab-reclaiming-words-can-be-such-a-bitch

14 TEDx Talks (2017). *Why You Need to Be a Bitch: Tabatha Coffey: TEDxStLouisWomen* [Video]. Retrieved March 28, 2019 from https://www.youtube.com/watch?v=OUmFdTHTD8M

15 "About Us," Bitch Media, Accessed March 28, 2019, https://www.bitchmedia.org/about-us

16 Joreen, "The BITCH Manifesto," Duke University Libraries, Accessed January 24, 2019, https://library.duke.edu/digitalcollections/wlmpc_wlmms01012/

17 Deborah Tannen, *Talking From 9 to 5: Women and Men at Work* (New York, William Morrow, 1994)

18 Sheryl Sandberg, *Lean In: Women, Work, and the Will to Lead* (New York, Alfred A. Knopf, 2013).

Chapter 2: The Stigma: Respect Versus Likability

19 *Wikipedia*, s.v. "What Are Little Boys Made of?" last modified August 29, 2019, https://en.wikipedia.org/wiki/What_Are_Little_Boys_Made_Of%3F

20 Tannen, *Talking From 9 to 5: Women and Men at Work*, ebook location 3220.

21 "Vocal Fry Hurts Women in the Labor Market," EurekAlert!, May 28, 2104, https://www.eurekalert.org/pub_releases/2014-05/uom-vfh052714.php

22 *Do You Suffer From 'Bitchy Resting Face'?* (2013)[Video]. Retrieved June 7, 2019 from https://www.youtube.com/watch?v=Xf-zXyfO7X8

23 "Throwing Shade: The Science of Resting Bitch Face," RBF, Accessed June 7, 2019, https://www.testrbf.com/content/throwing-shade-science-resting-bitch-face

24 https://testrbf.com/

25 Luvvie Ajayi: TEDWomen (2017). *Get Comfortable with Being Uncomfortable* [Video]. Retrieved June 7, 2019 from https://www.ted.com/talks/luvvie_ajayi_get_comfortable_with_being_uncomfortable?language=en

26 Tannen, *Talking From 9 to 5: Women and Men at Work*

Chapter 3: Recognizing Risk

27 https://www.bitchstigma.com/community/

Chapter 4: Bitch Privilege and Intersectionality

28 Kimberle Crenshaw, "Demarginalizing the Intersection of Race and Sex: A Black Feminist Critique of Antidiscrimination Doctrine, Feminist Theory and Antiracist Politics," *University of Chicago Legal Forum*: Vol. 1989: Iss. 1, Article 8. Available at: https://chicagounbound.uchicago.edu/cgi/viewcontent.cgi?article=1052&context=uclf

Chapter 5: The Bitch Spectrum

29 Sarah Ware, "Are You Suffering From Goldilocks Syndrome?" *Forbes*, October 1, 2013, https://www.forbes.com/sites/yec/2013/10/01/are-you-suffering-from-goldilocks-syndrome/

30 "So You Agree, You Think You're Really Pretty" *Mean Girls* (2017)[Video]. Retrieved June 14, 2019 from https://www.youtube.com/watch?v=d251b3X3YW4

Chapter 6: Toxic Bitch Behavior

31 Kat Blaque, Twitter Post, June 9, 2018, 8:59 PM, https://twitter.com/kat_blaque/status/1005615394701258752

Chapter 8: Who Gets to Decide If You're being a Toxic Bitch or a Bold Badass?

32 Deborah Tannen, *You Just Don't Understand: Women and Men in Conversation*, (New York, William Morrow, 1990), 182.Chapter 9: Sitting with Discomfort—Good Pain is Transformative

33 *Agents of S.H.I.E.L.D.* "Principia," Season 5, episode 13. Directed by Brad Turner. Written by Craig Titley. ABC, March 16, 2018.

34 Sandra Restrepo, dir., *The Call to Courage*, 2019, https://www.netflix.com/title/81010166

Chapter 10: Your Inner Doomsday Machine

35 Sandra Restrepo, dir., *The Call to Courage*, 2019, https://www.netflix.com/title/81010166

36 Valerie Young, Ed.D., *The Secret Thoughts of Successful Women* (New York, Crown Business, 2011).

37 "Take a Deep Breath," The American Insitute of Stress, Accessed August 9, 2019 https://www.stress.org/take-a-deep-breath

38 Gina Razón, Interview by Kali Williams. Personal interview, Denver, Colorado.

Chapter 11: Who's Got Your Back?

39 Jenavieve Hatch, "How the Women on Obama's Staff Made Sure Their Voices Were Heard," *HuffPost*, September 14, 2016, https://www.huffpost.com/entry/how-the-women-on-obamas-staff-made-sure-their-voices-were-heard_n_57d94d9fe4b0aa4b722d79fe

40 Jessica Bennett, "Workplace a Bit Sexist? Welcome to Feminist Fight Club," *The Guardian*, September 3, 2016, https://www.theguardian.com/lifeandstyle/2016/sep/03/workplace-sexist-feminist-fight-club

41 Anne Friedman, "Shine Theory: Why Powerful Women Make the Greatest Friends," *The Cut*, May 31, 2013, https://www.thecut.com/2013/05/shine-theory-how-to-stop-female-competition.html

42 Shanta Nelson, "The 3 Requirements of All Healthy Friendships," *HuffPost*, February 28, 2017, https://www.huffpost.com/entry/the-3-requirements-of-all-healthy-friendships_b_58b6153fe4b0658fc20f9b64?guccounter=1

Chapter 12: Building Confidence

43 Saul McLeod, "Pavlov's Dogs," Simply Psychology, 2018, https://www.simplypsychology.org/pavlov.html

44 Kim Elsesser, "Power Posing is Back: Amy Cuddy Successfully Refutes Criticism," *Forbes*, April 3, 2018, https://www.forbes.com/sites/kimelsesser/2018/04/03/power-posing-is-back-amy-cuddy-successfully-refutes-criticism/#5fc77d593b8e

45 Scottie Andrew and Nadeem Muaddi, "Megan Rapinoe Strikes an Epic Pose After Scoring Against France in the Women's World Cup. The Internet Goes Wild," June 29, 2019, https://www.cnn.com/2019/06/29/football/megan-rapinoe-soccer-france-trnd/index.html

46 "Beyoncé is Sasha Fierce," Oprah.com, November 13, 2008, http://www.oprah.com/oprahshow/beyonces-alter-ego/all

Chapter 13: Structure Supports Spontaneity

47 Brian Timoney, "How to Develop Your Sense Memory," Brian Timoney Actor's Studio, August 8, 2016, https://www.briantimoneyacting.co.uk/develop-sense-memory/

Chapter 14: Your Most Confident Self

48 Frank Niles, Ph.D., "How to Use Visualization to Achieve Your Goals," *HuffPost*, August 17, 2011, https://www.huffpost.com/entry/visualization-goals_b_878424

Chapter 16: Eliminating Soft Language

49 https://chrome.google.com/webstore/detail/just-not-sorry-the-gmail/fmegmibednnlgojepmidhlhpjbppml ci

Chapter 17: Dealing with Mansplainers and Conversational Bulldozers

50 Rebecca Solnit, "The Archipelago of Arrogance," TomDispatch, August 19, 2012, http://www.tomdispatch.com/blog/175584/

51 Tannen, *Talking From 9 to 5: Women and Men at Work*, ebook location 472.

52 Kieran Snyder, "How to Get Ahead as a Woman in Tech: Interrupt Men," *Slate*, July 23, 2014, https://slate.com/human-interest/2014/07/study-men-interrupt-women-more-in-tech-workplaces-but-high-ranking-women-learn-to-interrupt.html

53 Deborah Tannen, *You Just Don't Understand: Women and Men in Conversation*, 189.

54 Eddie Wrenn, "The Great Gender Debate: Men Will Dominate 75% of the Conversation During Conference Meetings, Study Suggests," *Daily Mail*, September 19, 2012, https://www.dailymail.co.uk/sciencetech/article-2205502/The-great-gender-debate-Men-dominate-75-conversation-conference-meetings-study-suggests.html

55 http://arementalkingtoomuch.com/

Made in the USA
Monee, IL
06 April 2021

64981543R00144